D0066078

c a t

cat

ANDREW EDNEY

wild cats and pampered pets

WATSON-GUPTILL
PUBLICATIONS
New York

Copyright © by The Ivy Press Limited 1999

First published in the United States in 1999
by WATSON-GUPTILL PUBLICATIONS
a division of BPI Communications, Inc.
1515 Broadway, New York, NY 10036

Art Director: PETER BRIDGEWATER
Editorial Director: SOPHIE COLLINS
Designer: CLARE BARBER
Project Manager: VIV CROOT
Project Editor: NICOLA YOUNG
Text Editor: MANDY GREENFIELD
D.T.P. Designer: CHRIS LANAWAY
Picture research: LIZ EDDISON

Library of Congress Catalog Card Number: 98-88860

ISBN 0-8230-0571-2

All rights reserved. No part of this book may be reproduced, or used in any form or by any means—graphic, electronic, or mechanical, including photocopying, recording, taping, or information storage and retrieval systems—without written permission from the publishers.

This book was conceived, designed, and produced by
THE IVY PRESS LIMITED
2/3 St. Andrews Place
Lewes, East Sussex, BN7 1UP

Reproduction and printing in Hong Kong by
Hong Kong Graphic and Printing Ltd.,
First printing, 1999

1 2 3 4 5 6 7 8 9/07 06 05 04 03 02 01 00 99

Page 2 illustration: *Pablo PICASSO Nude Woman with Cat (1964)*
Page 3 illustration: *ENGLISH Two Cats (13th Century)*
Page 4 illustration: *Gottfried MINDT A Cat in a Cage (18th Century)*
Page 5 illustration: *William Newzam Prior NICHOLSON Cat (1900)*

contents

INTRODUCTION
pages 6–9

PLAYING CATS
pages 10–49

SLEEPING CATS
pages 50–85

HUNTING CATS
pages 86–123

SOLITARY CATS
pages 124–165

CURIOUS CATS
pages 166–203

NURTURING CATS
pages 204–229

PIRATE CATS
pages 230–263

SOCIALIZING CATS
pages 264–309

WILD CATS
pages 310–341

SYMBOLIC CATS
pages 342–383

INDEX OF ARTISTS
pages 384–398

PICTURE CREDITS
page 399

ACKNOWLEDGMENTS
page 400

introduction

The world divides into those of us who like cats and those who are unhappy in their presence. It is a safe assumption that the reader of this book is firmly in the former group; and the group gets bigger every day.

In the last few years cats have overtaken dogs as the most popular companion animal in Western society. It is not so hard to see why domestic cats have become the ideal companion animal for modern, urban, workaholic society—although they still require plenty of care and attention, they are not as demanding as other species. Cats clean themselves, bury their droppings, sleep a lot of the time, do not have to be taken for walks, and do not bark!

Louisa Creed
Rosie on Ben Nicholson cushion
(1990)

It is easy to assume from this that interest in the feline species has only arisen recently. This is far from the case; apart from an unfortunate period in medieval Europe, when they were considered by some to be cohorts of Beelzebub, cats have always been a feature of domestic life. Probably the only difference is that in the past they had to work for their keep as pest controllers, and that the cat food industry did not exist. It was only in the late nineteenth century that the idea of keeping cats simply as companions came into vogue.

EGYPTIAN
Bronze Cat
(*4th Century* BC)

William
HUGGINS
Tiger's Head
(*19th Century*)

This book aims to show how cats, in all their forms, have been part of our lives for centuries—and how artists have tried to reflect this. It is true that cats do not feature in fine art as frequently as dogs, but their diversity in representational art is astonishing, and the many and varied examples seen in this book show that it is a rich seam well worth exploring. The technical difficulties of capturing "catness" are formidable. Anyone who has tried to photograph their cat in anything but a sleeping posture will know that they are not always cooperative models. On the other hand, cats delight in the luxury and efficiency of their own bodies, and their sinuous curves and flexible lines are irresistible to the artist who loves to work with a quick line to capture the essence of his or her subject. The texture, color, and patterns that are found in a cat's fur provide a lifetime study for some artists.

IRANIAN
Lion on Rollerskates
(1100 BC)

Here we see cats alone; cats piled in a heap; cats with people; cats with other animals; cats playing; cats with kittens; cats

ITALIAN
Benito Mussolini
(c. 1930)

hunting; cats indoors; cats outside; cats taking advantage; and cats bearing the weight of symbolism. And it is not only small or domestic cats that we are looking at. Few of us have the opportunity to see many of the big cats, except in captivity or on film, but their grace, elegance, and sheer power make them a natural choice for wildlife painters, and there are many wonderful representations in this book.

Any cat lover would be very hard to please if he or she was unable to find memorable images in the pages that follow. The illustrations range from bronze figures dating from thousands of years ago to imaginative depictions created in the 1990s, all of which just go to show that Felis catus*—Egyptian god, medieval devil, and now number one home companion—always lands on its feet.*

Crivelli CARLO
St. Jerome
(c. 1476)

playing cats

Frederick FRENCH *A Good Game* [**19th Century**]

Legend has it that cats are the offspring of lions and monkeys, with the monkeys contributing the play factor. Certainly the way cats play is one of their most attractive characteristics. We marvel at their athletic abilities and the grace of their movements as well as at the sudden, extraordinary release of energy that contrasts so markedly with the prolonged periods of rest and sleep that seem to occupy most of their time.

Louis WAIN
Cats Playing Cricket
(Detail)

Cats definitely seem to enjoy what humans consider to be play activities, but these sessions also serve a very useful purpose. What we see as play is the equivalent of "training" for cats. In order to catch its prey, the cat needs to be very sharp and agile, able to react quickly and accurately in a coordinated way; and in order to breed, to defend territory, and to maintain status and position in the local hierarchy, the cat needs to be fit and healthy. So, when cats are not resting, patrolling their manor, grooming, stalking prey, or breeding, "training" sessions take up most of their time.

◀ *Robert WARRENS*
Carpet Tacks (Detail)

Play starts in early kittenhood. A large repertoire of behavioral patterns develops from about three weeks of age. Kittens will knead their mother to stimulate the supply of milk. When weaning begins, the kittens start the first stages of socialization. They paw at each other to begin with, then they try batting their paws at objects and are stimulated to pursue them if they move. A whole battery of behavioral actions follows. Big-cat cubs and wildcat kittens behave in the same way, but in later life their "play" is usually deadly earnest. They must succeed at hunting to survive.

Jan BRUEGHEL THE YOUNGER *and Hendrick* VAN BALEN THE ELDER
Earth (Detail)

FRENCH
Lion in an Automobile (Detail)

The mother will direct the kittens' behavior towards hunting techniques as soon as their eyes have developed sufficiently. The most obvious of these is the "chase and pounce" technique. Kittens will chase almost anything that moves, such as a feather drawn away from them, and will show amazing agility with a table-tennis ball. They will continue to bat at moving aerial objects, such as a passing fly or a piece of knotted string suspended above them.

Complex social interactions follow in which hierarchical positions are established, if only temporarily. If a pair of cats is at play, one may stand on its hind legs in a dominant position with its forepaws outstretched; its companion may roll on its back, but still be capable of fierce defense. Pawing leads to play biting and sometimes real biting. One cat will ambush another or leap out at its owner. Then it may lie on its side, or stand and turn sideways in a taunting way, not unlike the provocative "I want to play" attitude seen in lively dogs. A quick sidestep is followed by rushing away at high speed,

Henriette RONNER-KNIP
Playful Kittens (Detail)

C. WILSON
Four Kittens (Detail)

with a sudden leap in the air. Then the cat may get itself into a favorable position to pounce once more and start again.

Cats also happily play on their own and often pursue imaginary objects, or turn on their own tail to chase it around and around. Most of these play activities are still very evident in adulthood in domestic cats.

Because a cat can move from a sleeping start to a highly charged state in an instant, it is incredibly difficult for artists to capture them accurately in motion. Photography offers some solutions, but the problems of representing mercurial feline movement remain; most artists have to settle for just-before or just-after images. The little cat with its tail in the air in Samuel Walker's (1802–74) *Two White Kittens in a Garden* (*see pages 16–17*) is a perfect just-before moment, and the pouncing cat in Horatio Henry Couldery's (1832–93) *Reluctant Playmate* (*see pages 100–101*) a just-after moment.

Judith LEYSTER
Laughing Children with a Cat (Detail)

WALKER

TWO WHITE KITTENS IN A GARDEN

[19th Century]

Pieces left out for the cats can also attract the birds. Most will keep their distance when there are cats around—even very juvenile kittens such as these—but magpies are almost as curious as cats. This one is ready to snatch its share, if it can stare down the kittens. One kitten watches to see which way things will go; the other is ready for a game: tail up, front quarters down, poised either to frolic or to flee.

Samuel Walker [1802–74]

MUÑOZ

CAT PLAYING WITH A BOWL OF APPLES

[c. 1920]

Shiny apples and a gleaming dish have attracted the attention of a curious young cat, apparently caught in the act of destroying what was an agreeable still life in the artist's studio. It is easy to read human traits into animals, but the cat does seem to have the appearance of a child in a "look at me, aren't I clever (or naughty)" stance. In any case, it is likely that everything will soon be on the floor.

Cuenca Muñoz

[fl. early 20th Century]

ROUSSEAU

PORTRAIT OF A WOMAN

[1895–97]

Rousseau is best known for his jungle cats, but the small cat in the corner of this work adds a homely touch to the impressive life-size portrait, believed to be of Rousseau's first wife Clémence Boitard.

Henri Rousseau

(Le Douanier)

[1844–1910]

" For he is of the tribe of the Tiger
For the Cherub Cat is a term of the Angel Tiger. "

MY CAT JEOFFRY

CHRISTOPHER SMART

(1722–71)

RENOIR

MOTHER AND CHILD

[19th / 20th Century]

Toddlers will always investigate furry animals, often unable to distinguish between the real and the stuffed. It is best if they are under supervision, as here, otherwise child or animal could get hurt. The cat has gone into the typical damage-limitation pose adopted by all sensible cats when in contact with small humans.

Pierre-Auguste Renoir
[1841–1919]

FRAGONARD

THE MUSIC LESSON

[c. 1770]

Here it is the humans who are playing. The music lesson was a favorite theme to show beautiful people at their leisure and, in most of Fragonard's work, a cast-iron excuse for flirting and dalliance. The cat's little area has been invaded by a stringed instrument, but it is sitting comfortably on a pile of manuscripts.

Jean-Honoré Fragonard
[1732–1806]

STEINLEN

SMALL CHILD WITH CAT

[1889]

The Swiss-born Steinlen was a prolific illustrator of magazines, but he is best known for capturing cats in every mood. Here he has caught the acute discomfort of the family cat wedged awkwardly in the loving, but clumsy clutches of a little girl.

Théophile-Alexandre Steinlen
[1859–1923]

ENGLISH
BE AT FRIENDSHIP WITH ALL AND THE DAY WILL BE FRIENDLY
[c. 1880–90]

The family pet fares much better in this charming Victorian card; the child holds out his arms to make a hoop and the cat seems ready to jump through as part of a game.

"I have noticed that what cats most appreciate in a human being is not the ability to produce food which they take for granted—but his or her entertainment value."

ROGUE MALE
GEOFFREY HOUSEHOLD
(EDWARD WEST)
(1900–88)

HAYLLAR

THE ROSE BUSH

[1870]

One of the artist's daughters determinedly shakes the rose bush, releasing petals for her kitten to pounce on. Hayllar had four daughters, all of whom followed him into the art business.

James Hayllar
[1829–1920]

RONNER-KNIP

PLAYFUL KITTENS

[c. 1900]

Although the rather sentimentalized style of Henriette Ronner-Knip no longer finds as much favor as it did, there is no denying her skill at depicting feline behavior. Here she shows two young kittens exploring a cigar box, the relative size of the box demonstrating how young they are; they pounce and clamber energetically, trying out their developing hunting skills.

Henriette Ronner-Knip
[1821–1909]

WILSON

FOUR KITTENS *(Detail)*

[19th Century]

In the first few weeks of life, young littermates seem to lack any sense of individuality and are quite comfortable treating each other's heads and bodies as part of their own; this group has the floppy ears typical of month-old kittens.

C. Wilson [fl. 19th Century]

“ She moves in little gusts and breezes
Sharp and sudden as a sneeze is,
At hunting Tibbles has no match,
How I like to see her catch

Moth or beetle, two a penny,
And feast until there isn't any! ”

MISS TIBBLES

IAN SERRAILLIER

(1912–94)

CHINESE

KITTEN WITH BUTTERFLY *(Detail)*

[20th Century]

The very delicate needlework of this Chinese embroidery is a clear indication of the high esteem in which cats are held in much of Asia.

DELACROIX

YOUNG TIGER PLAYING WITH HIS MOTHER

[1830]

Whether they are house cats or jungle aristocracy, young cats learn a great deal from their mothers. Play becomes modified for hunting purposes. Here a young tiger—now as large as his mother—paws playfully at her tail, reliving his cubhood. She, however, appears not at all pleased. Her look could be interpreted as mild exasperation at such "childish" behavior.

Eugène Delacroix [1798–1863]

“But when the blast of war
blows in our ears
Then imitate the actions of a tiger;
Stiffen the sinews,
summon up the blood
Disguise fair nature
with hard-favoured rage.”

HENRY V
WILLIAM SHAKESPEARE
(1564–1616)

GERMAN

ZIRKUS BEROLINA POSTER

[1984]

A dramatic circus poster from the former German Democratic Republic brings the frisson *of the wild into the urban jungle of "civilized" Europe. There is nothing but canvas between you and nature, ferocious in tooth and claw.*

BURKE

STATE OF BEING

[1996]

The artist believes that people are satiated with sensory experiences but his cat knows his limits and finds pockets of refuge from the madding crowd. Homage is paid to every cat's primary drive to inhabit cardboard boxes.

Jonathan Burke [b. 1949]

FOTHERBY

CATS

[1993]

Lesley Fotherby is famous for her cat paintings. Here a group of three cats, obviously from the same household, rests in its suburban jungle after a hard day's grooming.

Lesley Fotherby [b. 1946]

FRENCH

LION IN AN AUTOMOBILE

[1909]

Leo in a spin; this color print from the June 1909 edition of the Parisian magazine Le Petit Journal *shows an intrepid lion tamer taking one of his charges out for an airing.*

BRUEGHEL THE YOUNGER AND VAN BALEN THE ELDER
EARTH *(Detail)*
[1622]

Works by Jan Brueghel the Elder (1568–1625) were copied by his son, also called Jan. This is a copy taken from a series of paintings by Brueghel the Elder, known as The Four Elements (Earth, Air, Water, Fire). *In this copy of* Earth, *painted in collaboration with van Balen, the fruits of the Earth are brought forth into the center of a romanticized landscape. A pair of leopards plays, one with a small child astride its back. The Brueghels were ready to recycle many of their motifs: these are the same leopards, in exactly the same attitude but without the small child, that inhabit* Entry into the Ark *(1613), by the elder Brueghel. They also appear in* The Fall of Man *(1615), painted by Brueghel the Elder in collaboration with Peter Paul Rubens (1577–1640).*

Jan Brueghel the Younger [1601–78] and Hendrick van Balen the Elder [1575–1632]

CHARLET

YOUNG GIRL WITH CATS

[c. 1920]

Feathers always hold a strong fascination for cats of all ages and degrees of dignity. These long peacock feathers are especially mobile, allowing the young lady to lead her kittens in energetic activity and to catch the undivided attention of their mother.

Franz Charlet [1862–1928]

STEER

HYDRANGEAS

[1901]

Sometimes referred to as the "English Impressionist," Steer painted this portrait of his friend Ethel Warwick at the height of his skills. She wears the elaborate clothes of the artist's mother while she plays with her cat. Although the actual title of the painting is Hydrangeas, *it is the cat that is the focus of the work, bringing movement as well as a dark contrast with the sunlit colors in the room.*

Philip Wilson Steer [1860–1942]

VAN DEN EYCKEN
THE TABBY CAT *(Detail)*
[1920]

Slightly reminiscent of Henriette Ronner-Knip's work *(see page 27)**, this wonderfully executed tortoiseshell and white cat has her paw firmly clamped on the shiny spectacles. This is the sort of cat that comes and sits on the desk to help you with your work.*

Charles van den Eycken
[1859–1923]

“For every house is incomplete without him and a blessing is lacking in the spirit.”

MY CAT JEOFFRY
CHRISTOPHER SMART
(1722–71)

MARIS
INTERIOR OF A COTTAGE WITH A YOUNG GIRL PLAYING WITH A CAT
[1869]

The little girl's knitting wool is irresistible to her kitten, who worries at it like a dog. The white of the wool, the kitten's fur, and the girl's blouse enliven the humdrum gloom of the little cottage kitchen.

Jacob Maris
[1837–99]

MATRON'S KITTENS

"You have a cat ma'am, I see," said Mr. Bumble, glancing at one who, in the center of her family, was basking before the fire. "And kittings too, I declare." "I am so fond of them, Mr. Bumble, you can't think," replied the matron. "They're so happy, so frolicsome, and so cheerful that they are quite companions for me."

OLIVER TWIST
CHARLES DICKENS
(1812–70)

GÄRTNER
A BERLIN FAMILY AT HOME *(Detail)*
[1843]

There is a long tradition of including family pets in the formal group portrait. Here the young cat takes up a central position and brings a little action, if not frivolity, into a situation otherwise fraught with stuffy gemütlichkeit.

Eduard Gärtner [1801–77]

JBOudry

OUDRY

THE MONKEY AND THE CAT *(Detail)*

[1739]

This painting is based on La Fontaine's fable The Cat and the Monkey, *more an expression of manipulation and deception than of play. The cat has been flattered by the monkey for his ability to "pull chestnuts from the fire." As the monkey then eats all the chestnuts, the cat gains nothing; he is literally a "cat's paw." Oudry remains closer to the original of La Fontaine's fable than other artists, including Edwin Landseer (1802–73) in his* The Cat's Paw *(1824).*

Jean-Baptiste Oudry [1686–1755]

WAIN

CATS PLAYING CRICKET

[c. 1920]

Wain was very prolific and his cats are immediately recognizable. Most of them are seen in human situations or performing human activities, but they remain very feline. Earlier works show them in nothing but their natural fur, but later works dress them in appropriate sportswear. Wain's sporting cats were also shown playing golf, soccer, and tennis.

Louis Wain [1860–1939]

LEYSTER
LAUGHING CHILDREN
WITH A CAT *(Detail)*
[1629]

This work by Leyster, who was a pupil of Franz Hals (c. 1581–1666), has much in common with her Boy and a Girl *(c. 1650), an allegory of folly probably painted about the same time, in which another small cat is in a similar situation. The children are laughing, while the cat looks resigned to its fate. It was almost certainly painted quite independently of the children; no cat would stay in that position for long.*

Judith Leyster [1609–60]

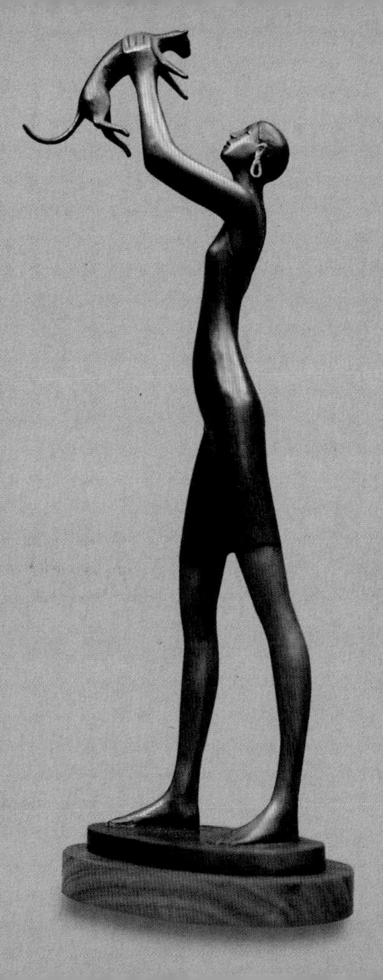

"When I play with my cat, who knows whether she is not amusing herself with me more than I with her?"

ESSAYS
MICHEL DE MONTAIGNE
(1533–92)

LEHMANN
LADY WITH A CAT
[1982]

In this sinuous bronze, the woman's own feline form is punctuated by the tenderly held cat, creating the elegance of a single sculptural line.

Craig Lehmann [b. 1953]

BLAIN

CATS AND A PARROT

[Undated]

Three bemused, beribboned kittens outstare a pensive parrot in this lithograph. Could they be the goddesses Hera, Athena, and Aphrodite in feline form, awaiting the judgement of a parrot-like Paris (the handsome prince of Troy), shown clutching the prized golden apple and pondering on who is the fairest of them all? (According to Greek myth, Aphrodite won.)

H. Blain [Dates Unknown]

WARRENS

CARPET TACKS

[1984]

Here the roles are reversed. The human performs amazing feats of bodily dexterity, which the cat seems to find extraordinarily amusing.

Robert Warrens [b. 1933]

sleeping cats

Franz MARC *Cat on a Yellow Pillow [1912]*

Cats are sprint animals; they expend lots of energy over short periods of intense activity in order to catch their fast-moving prey. Most of the remaining time is spent in far less frantic, energy-conserving activities, of which sleeping and resting are the most time consuming. To their owners, cats may appear to sleep—or at least doze—all day. This is misleading. As their prey is more plentiful in the early morning and late evening, their inactivity is more obvious to us during daylight hours. They are active when we are not. It is the same with the big cats.

Judy CHICAGO
Poppy (Detail from Autobiography of a Year*)*

However, like warriors, cats need to take advantage of every opportunity to rest, so they have developed different levels of sleep in order to maximize their chances. The more superficial levels are what we know as "catnapping." This begins by simply sitting in repose in an upright position, with the forepaws neatly placed to the front and the tail straight out behind. In a more relaxed state, the tail is tucked around the side. For this and the next stage, where the cat has its forelegs

◀ *Ralph* HEDLEY
Blinking in the Sun (Detail)

down in a horizontal position, the cat is usually located in a strategic, elevated position. Leopards doze like this on the branch of a tree.

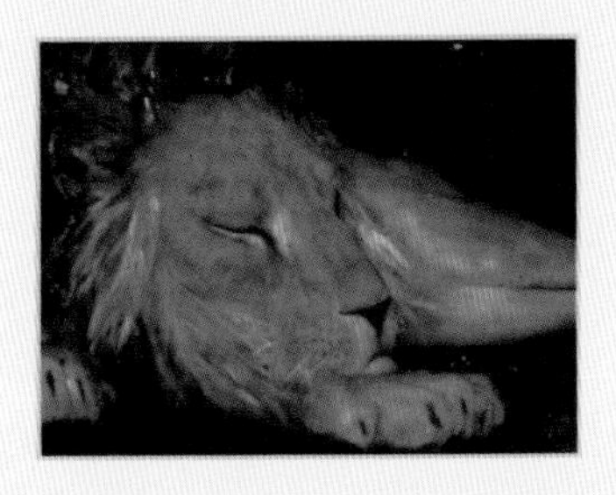

Gustav KLIMT
Fable (Detail)

A rather more relaxed, but still very alert, stage is reached when the cat curls up, often in a less exposed location. In a cool environment, the cat will curl up tightly, with its tail covering its nose. If it is warmer, the tail may be stretched out. The ears often remain very mobile to pick up all the rustling, chirping, and buzzing sounds in the surrounding area. Most cats keep their heads at an angle with their eyes partly open. This usually results in most of the eye being covered by the nictitating membrane, a protective third eyelid, which gives them a very eerie appearance. They are in effect asleep, but with low-level sensory detectors switched on so that they are able to pick up anything that might represent food or an approaching threat.

Pierre-Auguste RENOIR
Julie Manet with Cat
(Detail)

An intermediate stage exists during which the cat lies with its rear end down and its forequarters upright. In this way it can very quickly spring into action or spread out fully relaxed on its side. The deeper levels of sleep are normally enjoyed in the fully stretched-out position. Cats progress from one level of sleep to another quite rapidly.

Kittens spend over half their day sleeping and most of the rest exploring and playing. They will sleep after a feed, allowing their mother to leave for short periods to find food. Although cats are by nature continuous feeders, human care tends to modify their feeding patterns. After a substantial meal, the cat will find a quiet, safe, warm place, although its sensory apparatus remains active but at a lower level.

Because cats experience a brief period of rapid eye movement (REM) sleep toward the end of their deeper-sleep period, it is assumed that they dream in a way that is

JAPANESE
Sleeping Cat (Detail)

comparable with human experience. Although it is not possible to be sure about this, the electrical activity in their nervous system suggests that it might indeed be very similar. No one has yet discovered what inhabits their dreams.

On waking, cats either spring into action very quickly, if necessary, or go through a set process of coming to. This involves a good deal of stretching, shaking, yawning, and flexing of the spine. Any scratching that has to be done is completed before the fully active state is achieved.

The fact that cats spend about half their day in their various resting states makes it much easier for artists to capture their appearance in this mode. As a result, there are many more representations of cats asleep or resting than there are of them moving. Artists particularly well known for capturing such moments include Théophile-Alexandre Steinlen (1859–1923) and Leonardo da Vinci (1452–1519).

Alysse STEPANIAN
Is Peace Possible for a Social Being? (Detail)

“The wolf shall also dwell with the
lamb and the leopard shall lie down
with the kid, and the calf and the lion and the
fatling together; and a
little child shall lead them.”

ISAIAH 11:6

RIVIÈRE

APOLLO PLAYING THE LYRE *(Detail)*

[c. 1870]

In Greek mythology, Apollo was the son of Zeus, and the god of poetry and music among other things; it is said that he invented the lyre, which he played with profound effect. Rivière, the most respected animal painter of his day, shows a group of wild animals, whose savage breasts have been well and truly soothed by the charm of Apollo's music. These beasts include lions, leopards, and a lynx. Although peace prevails for the duration of the song, the big cats have made sure they are in the front row for the performance.

Briton Rivière [1840–1920]

JANOSOVA

THE DREAMERS *(Detail)*

[1997]

Sleeping cat and sleeping woman are both abandoned in languor, although the cat's pose indicates that it is more profoundly asleep than its mistress. This is artistic indulgence in an over-the-top romantic painting about the ambiguity of dreams, allowing the illogical placement of elements to invite the question "Who is the dreamer?" The only constant intended is the praise of sensuality.

Anita Janosova [b. 1951]

LEHMANN

SEATED LADY WITH CAT

[1983]

Luxuriating, sunning, and preening—the language, the mood, and behavior of the bronze lady and her strategically placed cat are inseparable, and equally appealing.

Craig Lehmann [b. 1953]

“Cruel, but composed and bland, Dumb, inscrutable and grand So Tiberius might have sat Had Tiberius been a cat.”

POOR MATTHIAS
MATTHEW ARNOLD
(1822–88)

GAUDIER-BRZESKA
THE CAT
[c. 1910]

Despite Gaudier-Brzeska's short life (he died in the trenches in the First World War), his influence as a painter and sculptor was considerable. Some of his most notable work was done from life in the London Zoo, where he drew pumas and jaguars. This pen-and-ink drawing could well have been the basis for a sculpture.

Henri Gaudier-Brzeska [1891–1915]

JAPANESE
SLEEPING CAT
[c. 1850]

The vision of contentment in this Japanese watercolor must be one of the fattest cats in art, although it may well be an exaggeration, almost a caricature. Its lethargy would have made it an ideal subject to paint—no need to dash down an impression, but plenty of time to perfect every pampered, silken hair.

HEDLEY
BLINKING IN THE SUN
[1881]

Early in his painting career Hedley, an artist from the northeast of England, established a reputation for his "skill in painting pug dogs, terriers, and cats." This painting, often called Cat in a Cottage Window, *is by far the best known of his works. The wonderfully tranquil tabby cat dozes in an open window, basking in the golden rays of the spring sunshine, its tail neatly placed to the front.*

Ralph Hedley [1848–1913]

HOLDSWORTH

IN THE SHADE

[1996]

Most cats have a talent for finding the right spot. The artist saw that his cat, Pete, chose a wheelbarrow's shadow, providing the perfect contrast between luxury and the rusty symbol of human toil.

Anthony Holdsworth [b. 1945]

STEINLEN

CAT ON A SOFA

[c. 1908]

One of several studies of adult cats in repose, this engaging work encapsulates the relaxation enjoyed by a cat in a favorite spot. Steinlen's cats are not always anatomically accurate but they capture "catness" as well as any artist since Leonardo da Vinci (1452–1519).

Théophile-Alexandre Steinlen [1859–1923]

◀ previous page

STEINLEN

THE CAT "CHIFFON" ASLEEP *(Detail)*

[c. 1910]

The eye says it all. As the animal catnaps, the senses are still very active. Two tiny flecks of paint show the eye sufficiently open to observe small movements in the locality. The ears are held back a little, as if scanning for the slightest rustle that could mean food.

Théophile-Alexandre Steinlen [1859–1923]

BURKE

WARM LIGHT

[1990]

Feeling at one with his cats in the studio, the artist knows that Calic likes company and feels safe sleepi in a patch of warm light on a cool spring day.

Jonathan Burke [b. 1949]

VERMEYEN

THE HOLY FAMILY BY THE FIRE

[c. 1550]

The Holy Family has returned from Egypt and rests by a fire. The cat, as is typical, has wormed its way into the best position, at the feet of Mary and right in front of the comforting hearth. It appears to be just a domestic cat, but may well be a symbol of laziness and sloth—forces that the young Christ will have to overcome.

Jan Cornelisz Vermeyen
[c. 1500–59]

KLIMT

FABLE

[1888]

This early work by Klimt, even before he became immersed in art nouveau, already shows his idealization of the female form. Here an Eve figure dominates the animals around her. The massive lion lies in deep sleep, while the cranes—symbols of vigilance—take frogs from the water vessels and dispose of them, to the intense frustration of the fox.

Gustav Klimt [1862–1918]

"The hind that would
be mated by the lion
Must die for love."

ALL'S WELL THAT ENDS WELL
WILLIAM SHAKESPEARE
(1564–1616)

BAXTER

PUSS NAPPING

[c. 1860]

A highly refined technique was used to produce the subtle texture of the cat's coat in this woodblock print. The cat is deceptively seen in a position of dozing; closer inspection, however, shows that it is very much in an action-ready state. The mice appear to be discussing some inadvisable, high-risk activity.

George Baxter [1804–67]

STEPANIAN

IS PEACE POSSIBLE FOR A SOCIAL BEING?

[1997]

For the artist, this painting is a play on opposites. Figuration and abstraction coexist. The image of the wild animal is in opposing relationship to the tame female figure; the stripes and drips indicate both order and chaos.

Alysse Stepanian [b. 1961]

" Like age-old sphinxes
crouched upon the sand
They strike majestic
attitudes to dream
And gaze at nothingness,
detached and wise. "

CATS
CHARLES BAUDELAIRE
(1821–67)

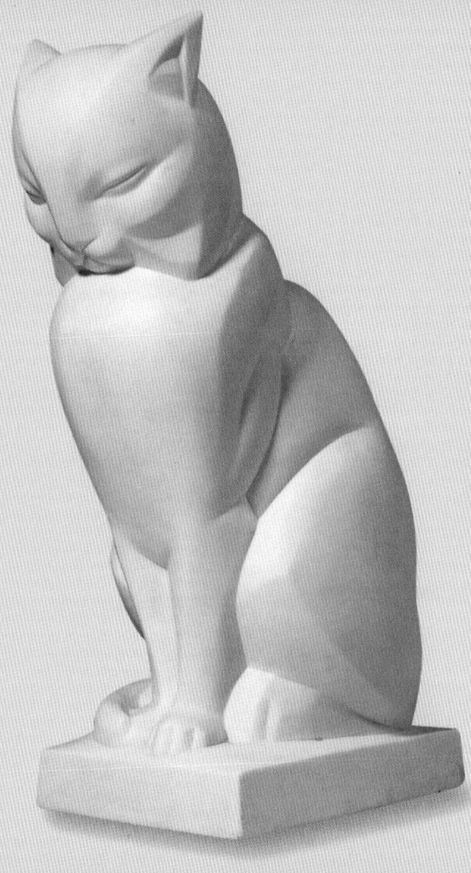

MARTEL AND MARTEL
STYLIZED CAT
[1925]

This piece of Sèvres porcelain is stylized in a contemplative stance with a distinctly Oriental touch. The cat appears to be dozing, but its ears are on red alert.

Joël and Jean Martel
[fl. early 20th Century]

GAUGUIN
EIAHA OHIPA
[1896]

In Moscow's Pushkin Museum this painting is artlessly labeled A Tahitian Interior; *the artist, famous for his retreats to the simple life, gave it its Tahitian name, Eiaha Ohipa, which means "doing nothing." Perhaps a more modern term would be "hanging out" (note the large exotic cigarette). In pride of place at the front of the picture sleeps the house cat; like all cats, it is an Olympic-class idler.*

Paul Gauguin [1848–1903]

LEES

NUDE WITH CAT

[1994]

During frequent shared studio evenings, the artist and fellow painters observed cats vying for attention with the model on the stand. In this study, a victor curls assertively on a corner of the couch for the remainder of the evening.

Richard Lees [b. 1945]

OLD HABITS DIE HARD

A cat fell in love with a handsome young man and begged the goddess Venus to change her into a woman. Venus was very gracious about it, and changed her at once into a beautiful maiden, whom the young man fell in love with at first sight and shortly afterward married. One day, Venus thought she would like to see if Cat had changed her habits as well as her form; so she let a mouse run loose in the room where they were. Forgetting everything, the young woman had no sooner seen the mouse than she jumped up and was after it like a shot; at which the goddess was so disgusted that she changed her back again into a cat.

VENUS AND THE CAT
AESOP
(C. 550 BC)

RENOIR

JULIE MANET WITH CAT

[1887]

Of the numerous cats seen in Renoir's works, this is one of the most joyous and relaxed. It obviously has complete confidence in its young mistress, who is the niece of Édouard Manet (1832–83) and the daughter of Berthe Morisot (1841–95), both fellow members of the Impressionist school, along with Renoir.

Pierre-Auguste Renoir

[1841–1919]

LEWIS

INTERIOR OF A SCHOOL, CAIRO *(Detail)*

[mid-19th Century]

While the children give their full attention to their teacher, the cat dozes lightly in luxury before them; perhaps it, together with the doves and pigeons, constitutes some form of teaching aid. The artist lived in Cairo for ten years in the mid-nineteenth century and his studies are a true representation of life there at the time. While not going so far as to deify the cat, the Egyptians had a benevolent attitude to such animals in the nineteenth century.

John Frederick Lewis

[1805–76]

LITTLE
VER-
ONICA
who likes to curl up in the bed

CHICAGO

LITTLE VERONICA

(Detail from AUTOBIOGRAPHY OF A YEAR*)*

[1993]

A study of one of the artist's cats, Veronica, which likes to curl up in the warmth of a human bed—but obviously only for a catnap, since the artist notes that she wants to finish the drawing before the cat leaves.

Judy Chicago [b. 1939]

CHICAGO

POPPY *(Detail from* AUTOBIOGRAPHY OF A YEAR*)*

[1993]

A closely observed cat, with one eye a little less closed than the other. The drawing bears the inscription "Poppy is a very odd cat. She doesn't like people very much and it took five years before we could pet her very soft fur." Much would depend on her early experiences. Cats that have not been socialized as kittens may not be pet-able at all. Others, which may have had frightening experiences, could take a long time to accept handling. The artist's patience and gentle approach are to her credit.

Judy Chicago [b. 1939]

SHIRLEY-FOX

LESSON IN THE GARDEN

[1900]

Another lesson with a cat relaxing nearby, in contrast with the Egyptian scene (see page 79). *Cats aim to be at once in the middle of any action (in case there might be food) and remote from any hurly-burly, with a cozy bed to lounge on.*

Ada Shirley-Fox [fl. c.1888–1940]

MARTINEAU

A GIRL WITH A CAT

[1860]

The child's cheek is rosy with sleep; the cat, a mature beast, is not really sleeping but bears the resigned expression of the family pet that has been cuddled to excess.

Robert Braithwaite Martineau [1826–69]

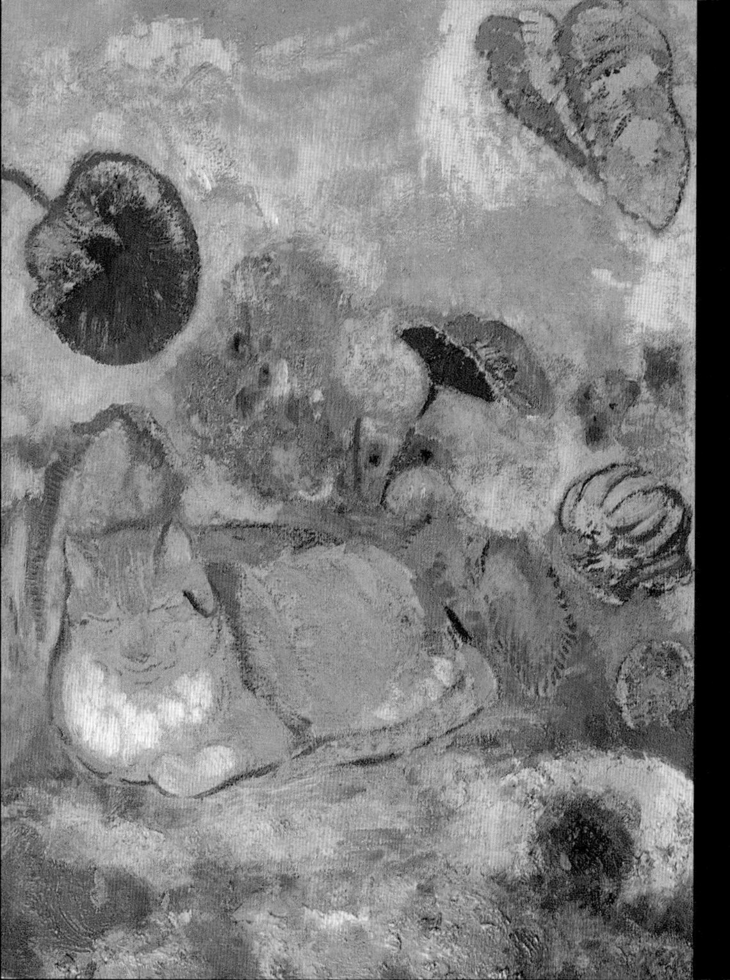

“Cats sleep fat
They spread comfort beneath them
Like a good mat
As if they picked the place
And then sat
You walk round one
As if he were the City Hall
After that.”

CATALOGUE
ROSALIE MOORE
(20TH CENTURY)

REDON
BAZON
[c. 1905]

Redon was one of the principal Symbolist painters of nineteenth-century France, but this warm and affectionate portrait of his sleeping cat belongs to his more straightforward style.

Odilon Redon
[1840–1916]

STEINLEN
RECUMBENT CAT
[1898]

Another resting cat from the master cat painter. Here the cat hovers between idleness, and activity.

Théophile-Alexandre Steinlen [1859–1923]

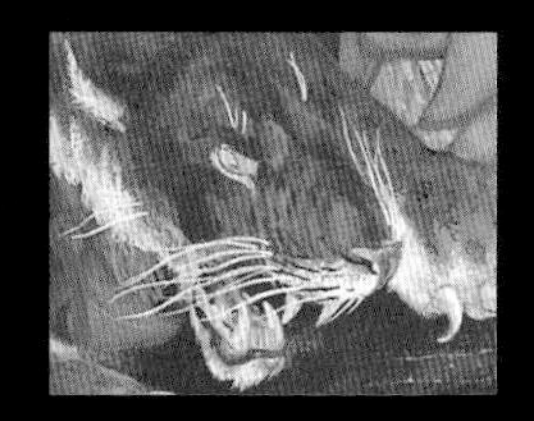

hunting cats

Paizs Goebel JENO *In the Jungle [1939]*

Jean Boe NIESTLE
Wild Cats (Detail)

Cats are strict carnivores and by nature continuous feeders, taking small amounts of food at every opportunity. In the wild, they fulfill their dietary needs by hunting, so they are designed for very efficient predatory activity. Much of this behavior is innate. Wildcat cubs and kittens born to a "hunting" mother learn the refinements at an early age. Kittens that have no such tuition still show predatory behavior, but to a less effective extent. If they are not taught to hunt, they will not teach their own young, and the skill is lost.

From around three weeks of age, the mother cat (queen) begins to direct her kittens' play behavior into something more productive than just aimless swiping and pouncing. At first they are encouraged to investigate dead prey. Then the process of despatching dazed and debilitated prey provided by the mother is perfected. The kitten learns to bite through the nape of the neck (and thus the spinal cord) to kill the prey so that it is ready to eat.

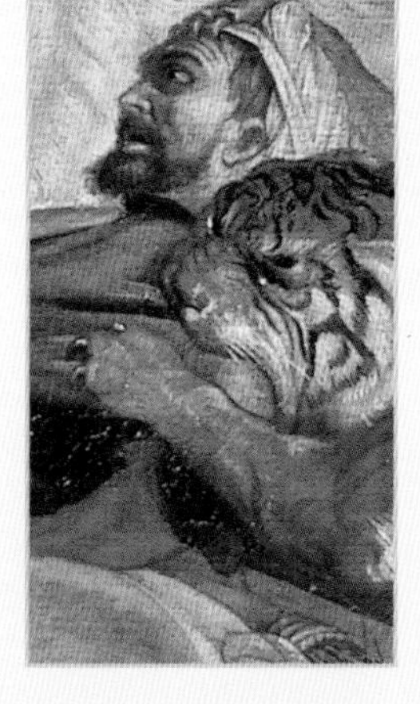

Peter Paul RUBENS ▶
Tiger and Leopard Hunt (Detail)

At the end of the weaning process, the queen takes her kittens with her as she hunts for prey. By the time a cat is ready to "go solo," it will have developed the finer points of finding enough food to survive. However, it is likely to kill only the kind of prey that it has seen its mother tackle; this explains why some cats only ever try to kill socks or balls of yarn.

The hunting technique involves patrolling home territory, a great deal of patient sitting in wait, reacting to noises, such as rustling and squeaking, and moving very rapidly in response to sudden movements. The cat's teeth are ideal for grasping and biting, but not for chewing. Their eyes are wonderfully adapted to make the best use of the reduced amount of light available when their prey are most active, and their claws remain sharp by being retractable. Finally, an extraordinary athletic ability and agility puts cats at the best advantage over the prey that they pursue.

Horatio Henry COULDERY
Long-eared Rabbits in a Cage, Watched by a Cat (Detail)

ROMAN
Cat and Bird: Ducks and Fish (Detail)

The cat's approach is slow and steady, crouching as it advances to keep a low profile. Its pupils dilate to gather in all available light and its ears turn and twitch to pick up the faintest sound. When it is within striking range, the cat pounces to grasp and debilitate its prey. It is only when the prey is sufficiently dazed that it is safe to kill it with a bite.

SARAHIDE
A Dragon and Two Tigers (Detail)

Mice, shrews, and other small mammals are the usual targets. Airborne prey are much more evasive, although a few cats catch birds and butterflies regularly. Others may take fledglings or birds injured on the roadside. Even rarer are cats that take fish. Although a few try fishing in shallow waters, most cats dislike getting wet; the exceptions are tigers and Turkish Van cats, which like to swim.

The innate drive to chase tiny, rapidly moving objects has little to do with hunger. Well-fed cats still show plenty of

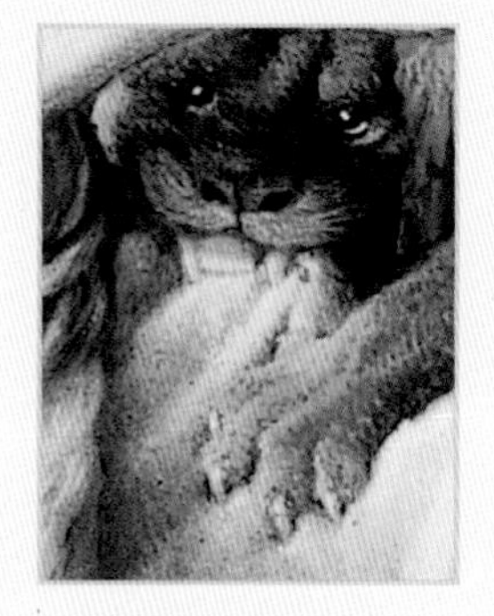

George Stubbs
Horse Attacked by a Lion (Detail)

predatory behavior, since they need to be ready for such activity. Really hungry cats tend to scavenge rather than hunt.

The majority of domestic cats are solitary hunters and operate by stealth and ambush. Some of the larger wildcats have different habits. Lions live in small family groups (prides), but it is the females that do the hunting, usually as a team. The male role is to protect the pride, and he always eats first. The cheetah is the only member of the cat family that relies on sheer speed to outrun its prey.

Horatio Henry Couldery
Reluctant Playmate (Detail)

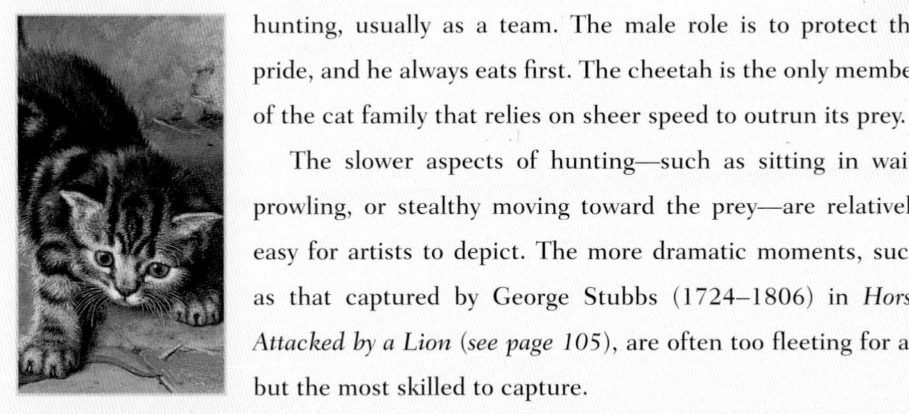

The slower aspects of hunting—such as sitting in wait, prowling, or stealthy moving toward the prey—are relatively easy for artists to depict. The more dramatic moments, such as that captured by George Stubbs (1724–1806) in *Horse Attacked by a Lion* (*see page 105*), are often too fleeting for all but the most skilled to capture.

Henri Rousseau

ROUSSEAU

TIGER IN A TROPICAL STORM *(Detail)*

[1891]

Also known as Surprised!, *this work is the first of Rousseau's "jungle scenes," painted after he had retired as a tollgate official at the age of 40. It is the best known of a series of more than 20 paintings of what Rousseau saw as life in the jungle, painted in the modern primitive style. The half-hidden, bristling tiger is in the act of pouncing. It is found in a "jungle" made up of greatly enlarged versions of plants that the artist observed in the botanical gardens.*

Henri Rousseau (Le Douanier) [1844–1910]

" Tyger! Tyger! burning bright
In the forests of the night
What immortal hand or eye
Could frame thy fearful symmetry? "

THE TYGER
WILLIAM BLAKE
(1757–1827)

ADAM

DINNER TIME *(Detail)*

[c. 1870]

Cats will eat together as a group from the same bowl; however, if you observe them, you will notice that they follow complex social rules to determine who shall eat first and who gets the most.

Julius Adam [1826–74]

HEYER

WHITE CATS WATCHING GOLDFISH *(Detail)*

[c. 1920]

All Heyer's cats seem to be of the white long-haired variety. No doubt they were part of his family. These two splendid individuals are somewhere between states of hypnosis and frustration as the fish elude them.

Arthur Heyer [1872–1931]

JACKSON

STILL LIFE OF CATS AND A LOBSTER *(Detail)*

[19th Century]

In this rather surreal image, the cats appear to disdain the lobster (which has been cooked and so can no longer suffer); however, if you look at the front cat's forepaws, you can see that they are poised to pounce.

A. Jackson [fl. 19th Century]

COULDERY

THE FISHING PARTY

[c. 1860]

Three kittens find that all that glitters is gold in this case, unlike poor Selima, the cat in poet Thomas Gray's On a Favourite Cat Drowned in a Tub of Goldfishes, *which "stretche'd in vain to reach the prize" and met an untimely end.*

Horatio Henry Couldery [1832–93]

COULDERY

LONG-EARED RABBITS IN A CAGE, WATCHED BY A CAT *(Detail)* [c. 1900]

It takes a little while to notice the cat in this picture, until you catch the unblinking single eye in the corner. Cats will watch potential prey for hours. Remember Mr. McGregor's cat, which sat on the basket containing Peter Rabbit and Benjamin Bunny for five hours. Are the rickety bars of the rabbits' cage enough protection?

Horatio Henry Couldery [1832–93]

THE CAT

Hark!! She is calling to her cat.

She is down the misty garden in a tatter-brim straw hat,

And broken slippers grass-wet, treading fearful daisies.

But he does not heed her. He sits still—and gazes.

Jessamines drop perfume; the nightingales begin;

Nightjars wind their humdrum notes; a crescent moon rides thin.

The daybird chorus dies away, the air shrinks chill and grey;

Her lonely voice still calls him—but her panther won't come in.

THE CAT
RICHARD CHURCH
(1893–1972)

ROOS

EAGLE OWL AND CAT WITH DEAD RATS

[17th Century]

As Edward Lear (1812–88) knew, owls and cats have sympathetic traits, but there will be no pea-green boat or shared slices of quince for this pair; see how each has a firm grip on its own portion, and notice who has the bigger share.

Johann Heinrich Roos [1631–85]

COULDERY

RELUCTANT PLAYMATE

[c. 1860]

These kittens are at the stage where they paw at every small object that moves rapidly—in this case the tail of the unfortunate mouse. The pieces of straw and leaves may well have been similar targets. The mouse stands a good chance of getting away from such amateur hunters if they are diverted and let go of its tail. Later, the kittens' mother will teach them to despatch the mouse with an effective bite.

Horatio Henry Couldery [1832–93]

SARAHIDE

A DRAGON AND TWO TIGERS

[19th Century]

In Eastern traditions Dragons and Tigers represent the contradictory and complementary aspects of life: change and stability, motion and rest, light and dark. The constant interaction (which is somewhat aggressive) is what moves life on.

Sarahide [1807–78]

“The tigers of wrath are wiser than the horses of instruction.”

THE MARRIAGE OF HEAVEN AND HELL
WILLIAM BLAKE
(1757–1827)

STUBBS

HORSE ATTACKED BY A LION

[1769]

This is one of a number of studies of a horse being attacked by a lion. The scene is one of intense violence and is based on ancient sculptures.

George Stubbs [1724–1806]

ROUSSEAU

JAGUAR ATTACKING A HORSE

[1910]

At the end of his life, Rousseau completed his series of extraordinary jungle scenes with this dreamlike representation of a jaguar attacking a horse. The enlarged plants from the botanical garden, seen in many of his other works, are also featured here.

Henri Rousseau
(Le Douanier) [1844–1910]

ROMAN

CAT AND BIRD: DUCKS AND FISH

[1st Century AD]

Cats have found no reason to change their habits for the last two thousand years. Excavations of the houses in Pompeii revealed this mosaic, showing a cat about to deliver a nape-bite to despatch a domestic fowl. It could have happened yesterday.

DESPORTES
A CAT ATTACKING DEAD GAME
[c. 1700]

A still life can be brought to active life by the sudden appearance of a cat. The bird's wing could still be moving after death or wavering in an air current.

Alexandre-François Desportes [1661–1743]

"When food
mysteriously goes
Chances are that
Pussy knows
More than she leads
you to suppose

And hence there is
no need for you
If Puss declines
a meal or two,
To feel her pulse
and make ado."

A CAT'S CONSCIENCE
ANONYMOUS

GREEK

BATTLE OF THE GODS AGAINST THE GIANTS *(Detail)*

[c. 180 BC]

This Hellenistic Greek sculpture is from the Altar of Zeus at Pergamon. It comprises the fragments from a scene depicting the Gigantomachia, a raging battle between the gods of Olympus and the Giants fought among volcanoes, the serpent-tailed offspring of Gaia (Earth) and Uranus (god of the sky). The lion may be associated with the hero Heracles.

DELACROIX

LION HUNT IN MOROCCO

[1854]

The hunter hunted and, as far as North Africa was concerned, hunted lions out of existence in the late nineteenth century. Delacroix visited Africa in the mid-nineteenth century and may well have witnessed such a brutal scene.

Eugène Delacroix

[1798–1863]

“Can the Ethiopian
change his skin,
or the leopard his spots?
Then may ye also do good
that are accustomed to
do evil.”

JEREMIAH 13:23

LEUTEMANN

THE KING'S HUNT *(Detail)*

[1863]

This is a woodcut modeled after the drawing of the same name by Leutemann; it is one of a series of drawings that illustrate a book of stories from the ancient East. It shows the king and his retinue despatching leopards.

Heinrich Leutemann [1824–1905]

WINSRYG

THE FIRST TRAVELERS IN SPACE WERE ANIMALS *(Detail)*

[1983]

Early space exploration used various animals in order to study the effects on them. Here homage is paid to all the animals that gave their lives so that we might explore the mysteries of the universe. The spaceship has been painted like a house being run by animals and made of living parts.

Marian Winsryg

[b. 1941]

MARSDEN

STATUE OF A LION ATTACKING A HORSE

[20th Century]

A starkly-lit photograph that adds a sense of menacing drama to this eighteenth century statue by Peter Scheemakers (1691–1781), especially when seen in the context of its peaceful surroundings at Rousham Hall, Oxfordshire, England. The theme is a common one with examples dating from antiquity; the painter George Stubbs made a number of studies of the same theme.

Simon Marsden [b. 1948]

HARDY

RED PANTHER

[1990]

Hardy is an artist and tattooist who has developed the fine-art potential of the technique, with an emphasis on its Asian heritage. His paintings, drawings, and prints are heavily influenced by the colors and shapes of Ancient Egyptian art.

Don Ed Hardy [b. 1945]

RUBENS

TIGER AND LEOPARD HUNT

[1615]

This is a studio copy of Rubens's original painting, which was burnt in Bordeaux. It is not clear who is getting the better of the fight, but it would be extremely unlikely for lions, tigers, and leopards all to be found during one hunt, particularly together. Rubens no doubt studied animals in the zoos and menageries established by his royal patrons; he would certainly have seen a menagerie in London, where he was ambassador at the court of Charles I from 1629.

Peter Paul Rubens [1577–1640]

INDIAN

PRINCE SALIM SURPRISED BY A LION WHILE HUNTING

[c. 1600]

In this Mogul Indian painting, a noble prince beats off the attentions of a lioness; his fellow hunters seem to think that he can handle the situation well enough alone.

“They call me cruel. Do I know
if mouse or song-bird feels?
I only know they make me light
and salutary meals;
And if, as 'tis my nature to,
ere I devour I tease 'em,
Why should a low-bred gardener's
boy pursue me with a besom?”

SAD MEMORIES
C. S. CALVERLEY
(1831–84)

NIESTLE
WILD CATS *(Detail)*
[19th Century]

A pocket tiger with its prey; notice the head held high to keep the prey off the ground and the authentic grinning grip of the successful feline hunter.

Jean Boe Niestle [fl. 19th Century]

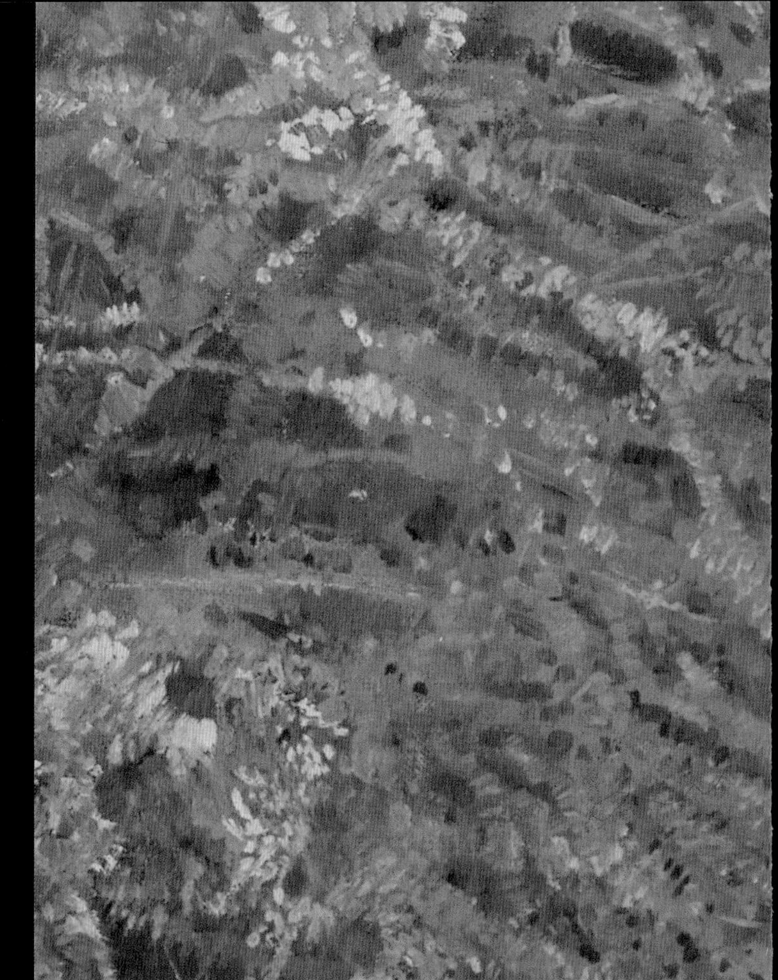

HOGARTH

THE GRAHAM CHILDREN

[1742]

The Graham family cat, one of the most famous in art, has climbed the back of the chair and threatens the goldfinch in the cage. Its mouth is open, demonstrating the Flehmen response to perfection: the cat "sucks in" odors so that they pass over a specially sensitized patch of membrane in the roof of its mouth; the brain then decodes the odors as taste as well as smell, exciting the cat and preparing it for the kill. The youngest child's hand gestures toward the terrorized bird, while his eyes are fixed on the cat.

William Hogarth

[1697–1764]

CHINESE

THE HISTORY OF SUMATRA

(Detail)

[18th Century]

This painting shows a native Indonesian cat. It is an attempt on the part of the Chinese artist to execute a landscape in the European manner, possibly to appeal to the sensibilities of European colonialists making inroads into the East at the time.

CRAWHALL

TIGER

[c. 1910]

Crawhall's watercolor tiger shows the influence of Impressionism. The dashing stripes and flowing curves evoke the sinuous nature of the beast; it might spring into action any second now.

Joseph Crawhall (1861–1913)

INDIAN

AKBAR HUNTING A TIGER NEAR GWALIOR *(Detail)*

[c. 1580]

This illustration comes from a Persian manuscript, the Akbar Nama, *written by the court historian Abu'l Fazl, celebrating the life and times of the Mogul emperor Akbar (ruled 1556–1605); here Akbar is seen on a lion hunt.*

WARD
A FIGHT BETWEEN A LION AND A TIGER
[1797]

Fur flies as rival kings of the jungle fight over disputed prey. Although very dramatic, this scene is extremely unlikely; lions and tigers, unless in zoos or safari parks, live on separate continents.
James Ward [1769–1859]

RUTHART

A PACK OF WILD ANIMALS ATTACKING AN ANTELOPE

(Detail)

[17th Century]

Of all the big cats, only lions hunt in a cooperative group. The artist may have seen leopards, tigers, and the other individual animals in a menagerie, but this scene is entirely imaginary. Even the antelope appears to be outside its normal habitat.

Carl Borromaus Andreas Ruthart [c. 1630–1703]

solitary cats

Christian PIERRE *Emma's Lion* [b. 1962]

Thanks to Rudyard Kipling (1865–1936) and his *Just So Stories*, the cat is popularly conceived to be an animal that walks by itself, a creature with an independent air. Cats are usually encountered alone, especially if they are tomcats, and the majority of homes impose singularity on their feline companions. For the artist, the lone cat carries symbolic resonance: independence, cool self-sufficiency, and mystery.

◀ *Ellen* BERKENBLIT
Untitled (Detail)

What is not generally known (except to those in multicat households) is that cats also live amicably in quite extensive communities. This is best seen in colonies of feral cats—these are either domestic cats that are living wild or offspring several generations down the line, living in farmyards, parks, or cities such as Venice and Athens. The basic feline domestic unit is mother and kittens; several such units, with unneutered tomcats to serve them and no human contraceptive interference, can soon build up into an impressive colony.

Rembrandt VAN RIJN
Lion Resting (Detail)

The cat prowling on its own is almost always searching for food. Part of this process is the regular patrolling and maintenance of its home territory. However, keeping competitors away is only partly successful in most cases. Most solitary cats have a set route that they take around the boundaries of their territory. They mark their scent on walls, fences, clumps of grass, and any other object that can be "labeled." Small sprays of pungent urine are directed at upright objects. Elsewhere, markers are left by rubbing the chin, spreading the secretions of small glands around the mouth at strategic points. Scratching at trees, posts, car tires, and so on not only sharpens the claws but leaves a scent from sweat glands located in the skin of the cat's foot. Every scent that is left has a characteristic pattern, which can be "read" by other cats in the area. The next cat to pass

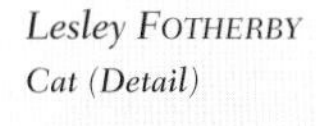

Lesley FOTHERBY
Cat (Detail)

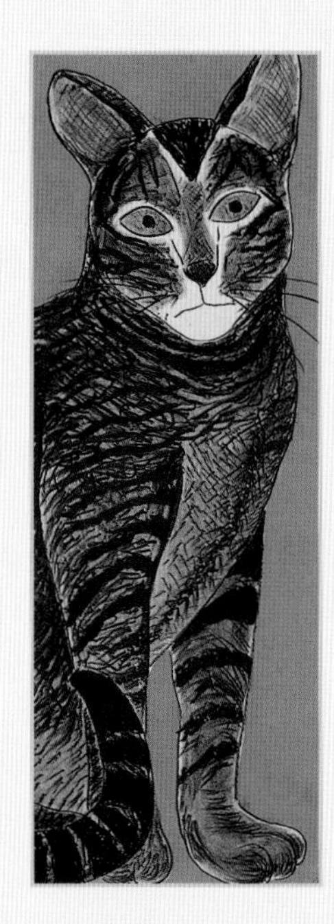

Joan Brown
Portrait of Donald (Detail)

by can tell who has been before, how recently it passed, what its gender is, and whether it is ready to mate. The second cat is likely to leave its own scent to override what it has found. In this way, territories can be shared without serious confrontation occurring.

When a solitary cat does encounter another on its patrol, a series of behavioral patterns emerges. One cat may adopt a dominant attitude and the other may take flight; both may take flight and thereby avoid any confrontation. If both compete for dominance, there is a good deal of hissing and spitting, and each will try to look as impressive as possible, arching its back and raising the hair of its coat, bristling its tail, turning sideways, and vocalizing in a strident way. They may spar and hit in a threatening fashion, but not necessarily make contact. At this stage, one cat may back down and break off the confrontation. Quite often the cat that concedes will wash

Kendahl Jan Jubb
Cat David (Detail)

Jean-Léon GÉRÔME
Tiger (Detail)

itself ostentatiously as a nonthreatening signal. It may then move quietly away to fight another day. In some cases, both cats decide to find something to do elsewhere, each perhaps believing that it has won the day. Just occasionally the situation is resolved only by real fighting, which usually results in injuries and abscesses for the feuding parties.

Most of the large wildcats lead solitary lives, meeting only to mate, with the mother rearing the cubs. The main exception is the lion. The males (usually no more than three) live with a group of lionesses and their cubs in a pride. Male cubs are allowed to remain in the pride until they are two or three years old, when they become a threat to the dominance of the existing adult males. A weakened, aging or sick male will eventually be overthrown and cast out of the group; an old lion, *sans* a few teeth, is indeed a very solitary cat.

Erich GERLACH
Cat at Sunrise (Detail)

ROMERO

SCAMP IN THE SNOW

[1995]

When creating his spontaneous graphic images, Los Angeles Hispanic artist Frank Romero often incorporates his studio cat, Scamp. Although Christmas in LA has never in recorded history witnessed real snow, the artist's imagination—along with the inspiration provided by his "best model"—produced this charming serigraph, or silk screen.

Frank Romero [b. 1941]

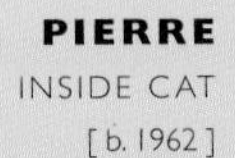

PIERRE

INSIDE CAT

[b. 1962]

Although a bright Moroccan moon shines alluringly outside, this cheerful home tiger looks happily settled in his own indoor, albeit extremely minimalist, jungle.

Christian Pierre [b. 1962]

STEINLEN

CAT STRETCHED OUT ON A CUSHION *(Detail)*

[1910]

Epitomizing the saying "cats know when they are on to a good thing," this lithograph is an affectionate portrait of one of the many cats that Steinlen cared for in the early years of the twentieth century. They were the inhabitants of his area of Montmartre in Paris. This one is meant to depict winter, as it rests in a position of both comfort and dominance.

Théophile-Alexandre Steinlen [1859–1923]

VIETNAMESE

THE TIGER

[Undated]

As it does in China and Japan, the tiger plays a significant role in the cultural life of Vietnam and its image is frequently shown in folk art such as this. Tigers are considered propitious and energizing, protective and warriorlike. In the context of Asian cosmology, tigers are the yang principle and dragons are the yin principle.

AMERICAN

THE CAT

[1840]

This imaginative, if disturbing, cat dominates the landscape, even without its body. Perhaps it is meant to be a bird's-eye view of a fearsome foe; it is certainly American folk art at its most monumental. It was evidently a popular motif. There is a version of this painting in the National Gallery of Art in Washington, DC, that may date from after 1840.

next page ▶

JUBB

CAT DAVID

[1995]

Not so much sitting on the mat as blending mystically with it, this orange-striped, green-eyed cat form is interwoven with a warm-toned floral rug, all making a busy background for the comfortable cat's pervasive Zen stare.

Kendahl Jan Jubb [b. 1957]

BROWN

PORTRAIT OF DONALD

[1985]

Handsome Donald is stylized, but still recognizable, in this lithograph made by his owner. His benevolent expression belies the ferocity of his tiger stripes.

Joan Brown [1938–90]

HUGGINS

TIGER

[c. 1880]

William Huggins specialized in animal painting and was an exhibitor at the Royal Academy from 1846. He seems to have had a minor obsession with tigers. They would have been a popular subject at the time; the second half of the nineteenth century saw the flowering of the British Raj in India (a major tiger habitat) and all things Indian were en vogue *in England.*

William Huggins [1820–84]

CREED

CAT'S HEAD

[1990]

This textured portrait is in fact a rag rug, the creation of Louisa Creed, flautist and self-taught rugmaker. The medium is ideal for rendering the density, movement, and subtle color of a cat's fur.

Louisa Creed [b. 1937]

HUGGINS

TIGER

[c. 1880]

Another of Huggins's dignified Panthera tigris *sitters stares out calmly at the viewer. Note the care with which the whiskers are recorded. It is curious that we can only see the head. The animal is as still as a statue and the glassy eye reflects the foliage that is more Kent than Kashmir. Could it be that this is the portrait of a stuffed animal, a trophy brought back from the hunt?*

William Huggins

[1820–84]

GÉRÔME

TIGER

[c. 1870]

Compared with Huggins's beasts, Gérôme's tiger throbs with sleek vitality, even though it's lightly dozing. The stains in the dust in the foreground suggest that the tiger has just enjoyed a good meal. Gérôme loathed the Impressionists; his paintings were always precise, realistic, and effectively realized. He was very interested in the Middle East and made several trips to Egypt, becoming renowned as a painter of things Oriental. It is unlikely that he saw a tiger there, unless it was in a royal menagerie.

Jean-Léon Gérôme

[1824–1904]

“Shake like lions after slumber
In unvanquishable number
Shake your chains to earth like dew
Which in sleep had fallen on you—
Ye are many—they are few.”

THE MASK OF ANARCHY
PERCY BYSSHE SHELLEY
(1792–1822)

REMBRANDT
LION RESTING
[1640]

If some artworks capture "catness," this pen-and-wash drawing on paper encapsulates "lion-ness" as no other. The work looks so simple, but it manages to express the lion's strength and belligerence as well as a noticeable distrust of all who approach.

Rembrandt van Rijn [1606–69]

Zampighi

ZAMPIGHI

TEMPTATION

[19th / 20th Century]

Little boys tempt their baby sister to a luscious pear while the cat waits on events. You could see this as domestic homage to Lucas Cranach the Elder's The Fall from Grace *(**see page 375**).*

Eugenio Zampighi

[1859–1944]

HOLDSWORTH

ANGLE OF REPOSE

[1987]

The cat pausing in the doorway is a serendipitous addition to the picture's mood and composition. Note the ears, pointed to attention. Whatever has lured the cat out of the warm kitchen is very interesting indeed.

Anthony Holdsworth [b. 1945]

“ O Michael
you are at once
the enemy
And the chief ornament
of our garden,
Scrambling up
rose-posts, nibbling
at nepeta,
Making your lair
where tender plants
should flourish,
Or proudly couchant
on a sun-warmed
stone. ”

GARDEN-LION

EVELYN HAYES

(DATES UNKNOWN)

FRENCH

THE CAT SAT ON THE MAT

[1893]

A cat caught behaving in an exemplary—if not educational—manner. The mat here is generously sized; all cats will find and sit on any strip of carpet, remnant of cloth, or scrap of paper.

Frederick French
[b. 1850, death date unknown]

JUBB

OSCAR 2

[1994]

Selecting one of her own cats, Oscar 2, as a model, the artist finds its dreamy appearance not so much a sign of serenity as an expression of the cat's contemplation of a food reward afterward, for all its hard work on the posing mat.

Kendahl Jan Jubb [b. 1957]

“ C’est un grand Monsieur Pussy-Cat
Who lives on the mat
Devant un feu enorme
And that is why he is so fat,
En effet il sait quelque chose
Et fait chanter son hôte
Raison de plus pourquoi
He has such a glossy coat
Ah ha, Monsieur Pussy-Cat
Si grand et si gras
Take care you don’t pousser trop
The one who gives you such joli plats. ”

MONSIEUR PUSSY-CAT, BLACKMAILER
STEVIE SMITH
(FLORENCE MARGARET SMITH)
(1903–71)

FOTHERBY

CAT

[1993]

Another mat-centered cat, but here the cat (a benign, standard-issue, domestic black and white) is the center of the work. It looks like a lovingly rendered portrait of an old friend.

Lesley Fotherby [b. 1946]

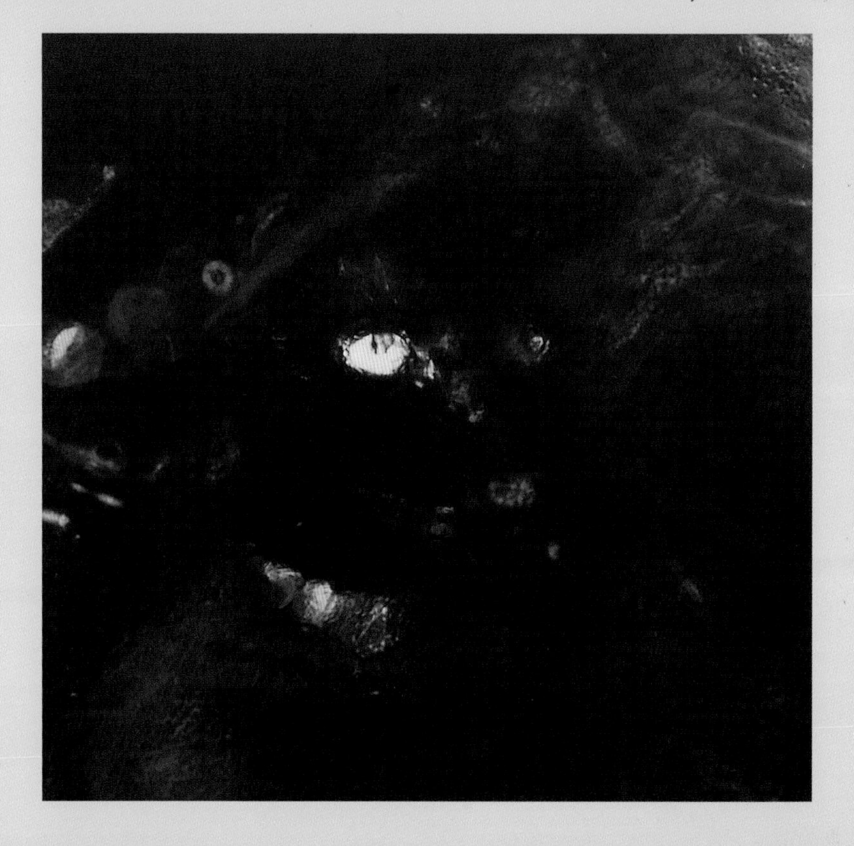

WEINSTEIN

UNTITLED (CAT)

[1996]

This photograph is part of a series entitled Interior Zoo. *It is the artist's attempt to give form to the collection of animals that inhabit the human psyche at the unconscious level—the frightening, beautiful animals that we release from their cages to wander through our dreams and fantasies.*

Margo Weinstein [20th Century]

GUTIERREZ

CAT

[20th Century]

In this work by a Spanish artist, Cat *is actually two cats. They inhabit a rooftop that is on the way to being an abstract design. There are echoes here of Manet's 1869 lithograph of Parisian cats, socializing on a rooftop.*

José Solana Gutiérrez [1886–1945]

STEINLEN

THE BLACK CAT POSTER

[1895]

Steinlen shows his talents as a graphic designer in thi[s] dramatic poster for a cabar[et] show in fin de siècle Montmartre.

Théophile-Alexandre Steinlen [1859–1923]

RENOIR

CAT ON A BLUE CUSHION

[1870]

Renoir painted several dogs on their own and a series of cats with young women, but there are very few Renoir cats painted without people included. This kitten is an exception. Although it lies on a comfortable-looking cushion, it still appears apprehensive. This could be due to the absence of its mother, or maybe just that the ribbon around its neck is too tight.

Pierre-Auguste Renoir [1841–1919]

JAPANESE

PAPIER-MÂCHÉ CAT

[Undated]

The technique of papier-mâché, "chewed paper," involves layering pulped paper with gelatinous pigment and chalky material. Papier-mâché is light but surprisingly durable. It has been a popular material in Japan for lucky charms and toys, like this fat little cat, just right for small hands.

BERKENBLIT

UNTITLED

[1992]

While cats do not walk around on their hind legs sucking sweets, the childlike creature here is still essentially feline. Note the curved paw and the action of the tongue.

Ellen Berkenblit [b. 1958]

HEYER

WHITE PERSIAN CAT

[20th Century]

Most of Heyer's cats are white long-haired (Persian). This one, however, has some cream markings. The breeding and showing of cats became widespread at the end of the nineteenth century and Persian cats, with their luxurious coats, grew increasingly popular. This individual has somewhat larger ears than one would expect today.

Arthur Heyer [1872–1931]

"The Cat. He walked by himself, and all places were alike to him."

THE CAT THAT WALKED BY HIMSELF
FROM *JUST SO* STORIES
RUDYARD KIPLING
(1865–1936)

GERLACH
CAT AT SUNRISE
[mid-20th Century]

Still bright-eyed after a night on the town, the black tomcat slinks home, where he will probably sleep all day. Cats' senses are designed to make them function better at night (when their prey are more plentiful and vulnerable). This has built up their enviable reputation as creatures of the night that harbor dark secrets and occult knowledge.

Erich Gerlach [b. 1909]

PATON

ALERT *(Detail)*

[1895]

This businesslike defender of the apple loft has been stopped in its tracks. The proximity of the gnawed hole suggests that the sound of squeaking mice has electrified the cat. The glossy tabby fur, like the watered silk from which it got its name, is well depicted here.

Frank Paton [1856–1909]

MUSANTE

CHEETAH

[1994]

An aura of mystery and ancient history provides a moody atmosphere for the cheetah, one of a series of animal icons assembled by the artist.

Ed Musante [b. 1942]

WOODHOUSE

SNOW LEOPARD

[c. 1920]

In its element on a high, rocky landscape, the snow leopard hunts alone. The dense, heavy fur of its coat helps to keep it warm in a very inhospitable climate in the mountainous regions of Central Asia.

William Woodhouse [1857–1935]

SCACCIATI THE ELDER

A JAGUAR

[c. 1700]

A lone jaguar pads warily through the ruins of a lost city, looking a lot more apprehensive than such a powerful beast needs to be. Perhaps it is the ghostly head in the foreground that has unnerved it—is it a statue or a grisly reminder of Aztec human sacrifice? The vague pyramid shape in the background locates the jaguar in Latin America.

Andrea Scacciati the Elder [1642–1704]

HANSEN
CAT
[1993]

This old cat is probably alone because it appears to have abandoned normal grooming practice and is obviously terminally grumpy about something.

Gaylen Hansen [b. 1921]

ATTRIBUTED TO
GÉRICAULT
LION WALKING
[c. 1820]

A leading figure in Romanticism, a movement from the early nineteenth century, Géricault painted a wide variety of animals. This attributed study of a lion may well have been painted in a Parisian zoo.

Théodore Géricault
[1791–1824]

"Cat! who has past thy Grand Climacteric.
How many Mice and Rats hast on thy days
Destroy'd?—how many tit bits stolen? Gaze
With those bright languid segments green and prick
Those velvet ears—but pry'thee do not stick
Thy latent talons in me—and upraise
Thy gentle mew—and tell me all thy phrase
Of Fish and Mice, and rats and tender chick."

TO MRS REYNOLDS'S CAT
JOHN KEATS
(1795–1821)

PALANKER
PAS DE CHAT
[1987]

The title of this work alludes to a ballet step; it is a pastel that the artist created in memory of her dead cat. Symbols abound in this image of two cats, a young one with an old one wrapped around it, signifying the whole life of the departed. The large urn contains the cat's ashes; a halo and cross suggested by the arrangement of the furniture in the room crown this elegiac work.

Robin Palanker [b. 1950]

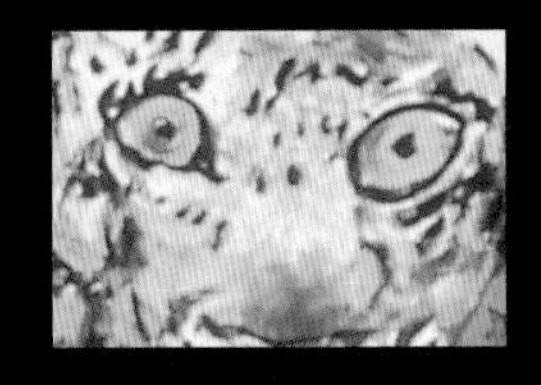

curious cats

Hunt SLONEM *Quetzal (Detail) [1984]*

Cats and curiosity go together like cats and cream. Why is this? As predatory animals, they need to be continuously aware of the availability of food supplies. They have to stay near their mother when young, find shelter, be aware of other animals, choose a mate in order to reproduce, and be able to find their way home. Other animals also do these things, but cats pursue them with notable single-mindedness and invention, exploring the most unlikely avenues with three things on their mind: Can I eat it? Can I sleep securely in it? And, if the cat is entire, can I mate with it? These drives

Jean-Léon GÉRÔME
Pygmalion and Galatea (Detail)

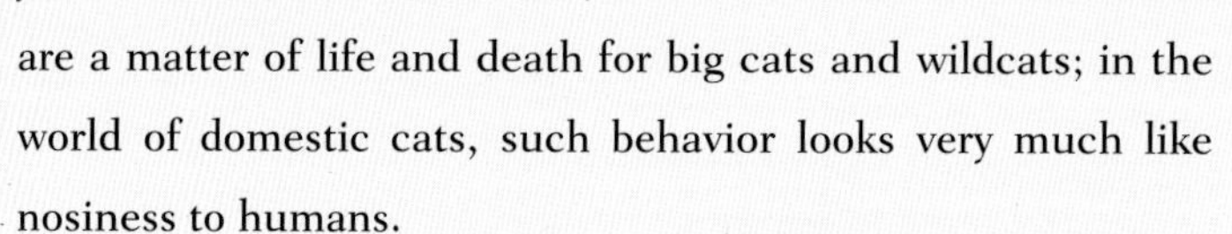

are a matter of life and death for big cats and wildcats; in the world of domestic cats, such behavior looks very much like nosiness to humans.

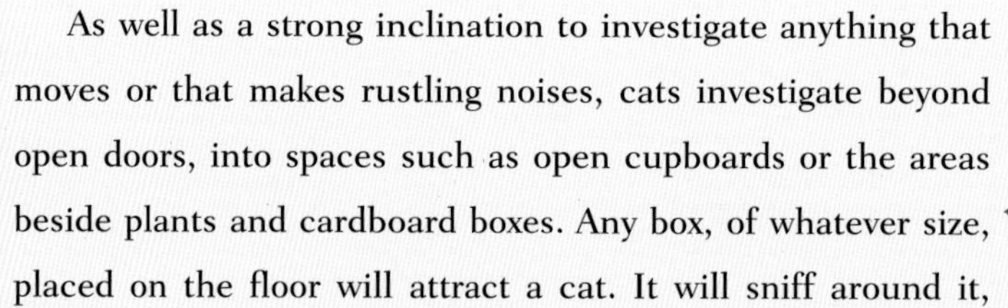

As well as a strong inclination to investigate anything that moves or that makes rustling noises, cats investigate beyond open doors, into spaces such as open cupboards or the areas beside plants and cardboard boxes. Any box, of whatever size, placed on the floor will attract a cat. It will sniff around it,

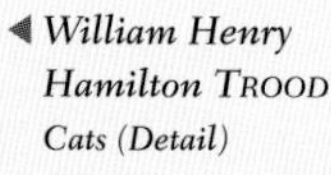

◀ *William Henry Hamilton* TROOD
Cats (Detail)

both inside and out, and nearly always sit majestically inside for some time. It is then an ideal subject for the observant artist. Presumably the cat feels secure and is able to keep a watchful eye on its surroundings. Even though many cats get themselves into difficult, even trapped, situations, they usually leave an avenue of escape, in case they are threatened.

Nicolas TARKHOFF
Black Cat on the Window Rail (Detail)

The urge to explore is underpinned by the cat's sensory systems, which are more sensitive than those of most other mammals. There is some 30 percent more sensory tissue devoted to detecting odors compared with the human allocation; the ears are very mobile, detecting sounds at frequencies 50 percent higher than dogs can; the eyes have little capacity to see colors, being designed to detect movement; and the pupils can dilate to pick up so much available light that what, to humans, appears a dark night is to cats just a rather dim day.

Alfred DUKE
Hesitation (Detail)

Charles VAN DEN EYCKEN
Cat with a Basket (Detail)

So cats are able to investigate their world thoroughly from kittenhood, and kittens begin to explore their surroundings from a very early age. As they become more mobile, they use their sense of smell to investigate everything they encounter. They show very little fear at this stage and remain under their mother's surveillance. As she trains them for an independent life, they develop their senses to a high level of acuity. Each kitten learns what to be wary of and what to look closer at.

Not only are all the senses finely tuned once maturity is reached, but there may well be additional qualities, outside our experience, that enable cats to survive. Of these, the ability to find their way home is the best known. Magnetic fields are probably involved. Although a range of around 7½ miles (12 kilometers) is the norm, much greater distances have been covered in many well authenticated cases.

Koyanagui SEI
Cat on a Rush Chair (Detail)

Most cats tend to stick to exploring their home range, which extends a little beyond their marked territory. Entire male cats have larger territories than females and neutered tomcats, partly because they have a powerful motivation to seek out females that are ready to mate. In the cat's territory, there is a social distance within which it will permit safe interactions. Inside this is a personal area, to which only those cats that are accepted are given free access.

A cat may proverbially look at a king, and most cats will inspect human visitors to the household to see whether they pose a threat, whether they have brought in any new, exciting smells, are carrying any food, are warm and comfortable to sit on, and whether they are likely to provide due attention and a major stroking session. Insatiable curiosity may be the reason why so many cats feature in paintings; there might just be something good to eat in that box of oil paints...

William Henry Hamilton TROOD
Cats (Detail)

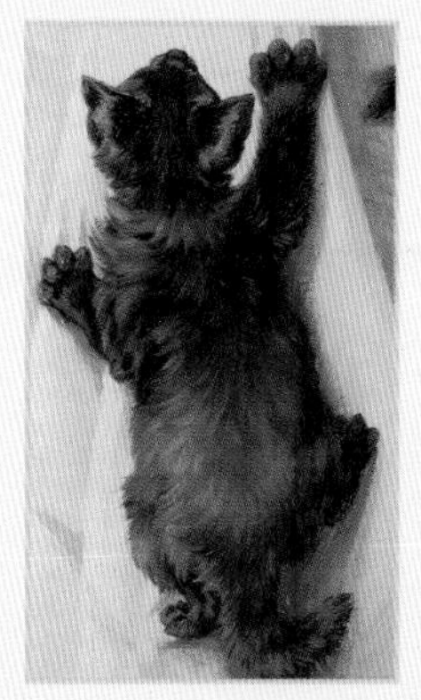

BURKE

CAGED VANITY

[1991]

The curious cat poking its head out of the drawer represents nemesis for the unaware birds that dominate the picture, especially the prizewinner in its cage. The bright colors and surreal juxtapositions in this image are as intriguing to the viewer as the birds are to the cat.

Jonathan Burke [b. 1949]

LE ROY

IN THE DRESSING-TABLE BOX

[c. 1860]

Kittens seem to be programed to explore the tangling potential of wool; these wreckers are in a style very reminiscent of the paintings of Henriette Ronner-Knip (1821–1909)

Jules le Roy [1833–65]

CHICAGO

TRIO *(Detail from Autobiography of a Year)*

[1993]

The feminist artist Judy Chicago has a passion for cats. She has shared her life with a number of cats, all of which she has painted. Trio's lack of part of a hind leg has not diminished her beauty or dimmed the intensity of her curious gaze.

Judy Chicago [b. 1939]

PFEIFFER

KITTENS

[1882]

This is a color lithograph for a children's storybook, illustrating naughtiness in the schoolroom. A warning of the danger inherent in such behavior is given by the needle that is dangerously near to the sleeping kitten's eye.

Wilhelm Pfeiffer [19th Century]

“If a fish is the movement of water embodied, given shape, then a cat is a diagram and pattern of subtle air.”

PARTICULARLY CATS

DORIS LESSING

(B. 1919)

BROWN

THE ADOLESCENT CAT *(Detail)*

[1983]

Joan Brown was the youngest member of the Bay Area Figurative movement based in San Francisco. She attempted to merge figuration with abstraction, as shown in this lithograph. A preference for Oriental art, with its simplification of nature, makes her model (a rakish young ginger tomcat with an inquisitive eye) a metaphysical symbol rather than merely a representation of a decorative style.

Joan Brown [1938–90]

MEIERS

SOMETHING UNFORESEEN

[1987]

The artist is influenced by dream imagery, which she renders theatrically or operatically. Here a big cat, possibly a cheetah or a leopard, cowers under a red sky lit by the baleful gleam of a thousand huge eyes, echoing the pattern in a peacock's tail.

Susanna Meiers [b. 1949]

VAN DEN EYCKEN

CAT WITH A BASKET

[1916]

Curiosity has got the better of climbing ability here, as the young cat extends its range, clambering rather awkwardly to investigate the secrets in the basket. The anxious grip of the back legs and the overall curve of the body suggest that the kitten is much higher up than it really is; older cats have more confidence.

Charles van den Eycken [1859–1923]

TROOD

CATS (*Detail*)

[1899]

Cats are willing to tackle very challenging obstacles to satisfy their investigative urges. These kittens climb the mountainous tablecloth under the surveillance of their mother.

William Henry Hamilton Trood [1860–99]

“Sally, having
swallowed cheese,
Directs down holes
the scented breeze,
Enticing thus
with bated breath
Nice mice to an
untimely death.”

CRUEL CLEVER CAT
GEOFFREY TAYLOR
(DATES UNKNOWN)

STEINLEN

CATS

[1910]

Curious—we? Cat owners who have transgressed some unwritten feline law are familiar with the attitude of these two cats: curiosity and disdain mingled in equal proportion. The same two cats appear with the same attitude in a color lithograph for a poster advertising an exhibition of the artist's works at the Galerie Bodinière in Paris in 1894.

Théophile-Alexandre Steinlen [1859–1923]

" Pure blooded domestic, guaranteed,
Soft-mannered, musical in purr,
The ribbons had declared the breed,
Gentility was in the fur.

I saw the generations pass
Along the reflex of a spring
A bird had rustled in the grass
The tab had caught it on the wing. "

THE PRIZE CAT
E. J. PRATT
(1883–1964)

KOECK
LADY CAT
[Undated]

Well-bred cats contain their curiosity. Only the twitch of her tail betrays this beautiful Siamese empress, set in a surreal landscape containing flowers, a shell, a bird—all attributes of Venus, the goddess of love.

Micha Koeck [Dates Unknown]

GÉRÔME

PYGMALION AND GALATEA

[19th Century]

The Greek sculptor Pygmalion has fallen in love with the statue he has made of a perfect woman, the milk-white Galatea. Aphrodite, the goddess of love, kindly brings the statue to life for him. We are witnessing the moment of transformation. The little black cat, which has recently given birth herself in the natural way, looks on in round-eyed amazement.

Jean-Léon Gérôme [1824–1904]

BATTEN

SLEEPING BEAUTY

[19th / 20th Century]

The well-known story of the Sleeping Beauty dates from seventeenth-century France. In this picture, painted in the prevailing Pre-Raphaelite style, Beauty's ginger puss sleeps on, oblivious to danger; it is no match for the lithe, dark venom of the wicked witch's padding black panther. Even the owl, representative of wisdom, is asleep at its post.

John D. Batten [1860–1932]

HEYER

AN UNINVITED GUEST

[c. 1910]

Two white long-haired cats very typical of Arthur Heyer's style show both opportunism and curiosity. Whoever has just left the deck chair has had their place taken without being asked. The other uninvited guest is the hapless ladybird. Heyer's cats are always well realized, retaining their individuality while exemplifying the essence of cat behavior.

Arthur Heyer [1872–1931]

CHRISTENSEN

FLIGHT INTO EGYPT

[1986]

While painting a languid nude model reading Proust, the artist also incorporated a cat. Is the reader searching for lost times? And is the cat a distant echo from ancient Egypt?

Wes Christensen [b. 1949]

next page ▶

ALMA-TADEMA

GOOD FRIENDS

[19th Century]

This picture is smaller in scale than the artist's usual epic paintings, and the protagonists are more homely, but note the classical costume, the marble surfacing, and the hint of a temple outside the door.

Lawrence Alma-Tadema [1836–1912]

"O tiger's heart wrapped in a woman's hide!"

HENRY VI, PART III
WILLIAM SHAKESPEARE
(1564–1616)

ROUSSEAU
THE DREAM *(Detail)*
[1910]

Painted toward the end of his life, The Dream *continued Rousseau's "jungle scenes" begun with* Tiger in a Tropical Storm (see pages 92–93). *The object of curiosity to one of the big cats, the dreamer lounges on an incongruous chaise longue in a typical Rousseau plantscape. The round-eyed jungle cats look fierce, but dream cats can do no harm.*

Henri Rousseau (Le Douanier) [1844–1910]

“If man could be crossed with a cat,
it would improve man,
but it would deteriorate the cat.”

MARK TWAIN
(1835–1910)

HOCKNEY

MR & MRS CLARK AND PERCY
[1970]

Central to the composition of this work, the magnificent Percy (actually Blanche) has a splendid presence. Its curiosity is fixed by something happening outside the window and it sits in the attitude of the bronze cats of ancient Egypt. Fashion designer Ossie Clark and his wife Celia Birtwell were seminal figures in 1960s London, and Hockney was a personal friend.

David Hockney [b. 1937]

HIROSHIGE

CAT IN A WINDOW
[19th Century]

Hiroshige, along with Katsushika Hokusai (1760–1849), was the master of woodblock printing. This example comes from the series Famous Sites of Edo: One Hundred Views. *The cat surveying the scene from the window is a bobtail cat, considered to be especially lucky by the Japanese.*

Andō Hiroshige [1797–1858]

TARKHOFF

BLACK CAT ON THE WINDOW RAIL

[19th / 20th Century]

All cats have an impressive head for heights and are able to balance on very narrow surfaces. This cat may have leapt up onto the rail to follow the flight of a bird or insect, to make itself known as ruler of the territory, or simply to have an alfresco meowing session.

Nicolas Tarkhoff [1871–1930]

JAMES

CAT IN THE WINDOW

[20th Century]

One of the favorite subjects for artists is the view from the studio window. Here the cat, apparently staring fixedly at something beyond our view, focuses on an area amid the Parisian rooftops outside the atelier.

Willy James [b. 1920]

"Cat if you go
outdoors you must
walk in snow,
You will come back
with little white shoes
on your feet,
Little white slippers
of snow that have
heels of sleet."

ON A NIGHT OF SNOW
ELIZABETH J. COATSWORTH
[B. 1893, DEATH DATE UNKNOWN]

BISSELL

EXODUS

[1988]

A Maurits Cornelis Escher-like (1898–1972) pattern of bats intrigues the cat in the foreground. Although the bats leaving a cave and the barren landscape suggest an ominous dark aspect, the cat grins at this macabre exodus as if it is a symbol of hope.

Robert Bissell [b. 1952]

GÉRÔME

TIGER ON THE WATCH

[c. 1888]

Gérôme was known to have visited North Africa and to feature many animals in his works, but this meticulously observed tiger was probably painted from the skin or from captive specimens. Note that the tiger's stripes are less well defined over the shoulder, which reflects the artist's thorough research and accuracy. What we see is not really our conventional idea of jungly tiger country, but the armies massing on the plain below have aroused the big cat's curiosity.

Jean-Léon Gérôme [1824–1904]

“ i wake the world from sleep
as i caper and sing and leap
when i sing my wild free tune
wotthehell wotthehell. ”

THE SONG OF MEHITABEL
FROM ARCHY AND MEHITABEL
DON MARQUIS
[1878-1937]

STEINLEN
THE CAT
[1910]

This charcoal and pastel study shows a cat stopped in its tracks by some distraction, such as its owner calling its name or the meowing of a prospective mate.

Théophile Alexandre Steinlen
[1859–1923]

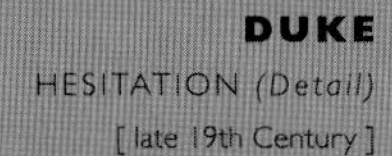

DUKE

HESITATION *(Detail)*

[late 19th Century]

The cat's curiosity overrides its fear of the two dogs, whose attention has been temporarily attracted by the flappings of a magpie in the house doorway. This genre of narrative picture, with a catchy title and animals enacting the story, was very popular in the Victorian era; even Edwin Landseer (1802–73) produced some examples.

Alfred Duke [fl. 1890–1910]

THE LONG CAT

Oh a cat's a cat. Babou's only too long when he really wants to be. Are we even sure he's black? He's probably white in snowy weather, dark blue at night, and red when he goes to steal strawberries. He's very light when he lies on your knees, and very heavy when I carry him into the kitchen in the evenings to prevent him from sleeping on my bed. I think he's too much of a vegetarian to be a real cat.

THE LONG CAT
COLETTE
(SIDONIE GABRIELLE COLETTE)
(1873–1954)

WEST
CHILDREN EATING CHERRIES
[1800]

Cats are always curious about what other animals are eating, even if they cannot eat—or don't want—the food themselves. Here one of the cats has obviously had a taste and rejected the cherries. West was an American painter who specialized in historical paintings. The children are adorned in classical dress.

Benjamin West [1738–1820]

DITZ

THE RADISH HUNT

[1996]

Trainee cats practice their pounces on anything with the rough shape and scale of their prey; here it is a chubby radish with a taproot like a mouse-tail and shoots that could just be mistaken for ears. Note the kitten's concentrated stare, pricked ears, and characteristic pounce-posture; the radish is doomed.

Ditz [20th Century]

ERLEBACHER

ODALISQUE

[1991]

The cat echoes the pose of the voluptuous odalisque. A classical preening nude is upstaged by her equally narcissistic cat. Erlebacher's work deals less with realism than with the inner meaning of the moody, sensuous metaphors that bloom from her subjects.

Martha Mayer Erlebacher [b. 1937]

SEI

CAT ON A RUSH CHAIR

[20th Century]

It is usually when it is a little chilly that cats curl their tail around their nose to retain heat. This cat has been in a comfortable position, but its curiosity has been awoken by something. Observe the Japanese version of a Vincent van Goghesque (1853–90) setting.

Koyanagui Sei

[b. 1896, death date unknown]

MEIERS

BIG CAT

[1988]

The artist specializes in dream-based visions. This work pays homage to her cat Olive, which finds immortality in this dream landscape where she's coupled with a garden snail.

Susanna Meiers [b. 1949]

“ Cats sleep
Anywhere
Any table
Any Chair
Top of piano
Window-ledge
In the middle
On the edge
Open drawer
Empty shoe ”

CATS
ELEANOR FARJEON
[1881-1965]

dique
Lehmann

nurturing **cats**

Jacques LEHMANN *Mother with Kittens [* ***20th Century*** *]*

Horatio Henry COULDERY
Playing with Mother
(Detail)

All young animals have a good measure of charm, but kittens have universal appeal. They grow up at a remarkable rate and mother cats (queens) have a total commitment to their upbringing. Young cats can be sexually active before they are six months old, and the gestation period lasts for around sixty-three days. As a result, litters can be born to mothers under a year old. However, queens normally start their estrus cycles as the days begin to lengthen early in the year. So most kittens start their lives in late spring or early summer.

First litters are usually restricted to one or two kittens. After that, five- or six-kitten litters are not unusual. Queens normally get on with the task of giving birth in a businesslike fashion and rarely need assistance. They find a place to do this that is best suited to themselves but not always the most convenient place for their owners. They readily foster orphan kittens or

William Henry Hamilton TROOD
Women's Rights—A Meeting (Detail)

Lesley FOTHERBY
Blue Cats Waking (Detail)

those from mothers that fail to lactate. Each kitten finds its own teat and is fed by its mother or foster mother for around eight weeks. Kittens weaned before this time tend to be less able to seek out their own food. Kittens that are born after a gestation period of less than fifty-eight days do not usually survive.

Up to the point that kittens are about three weeks old, the mother spends most of her time providing milk for her litter and cleaning them all meticulously. Lactation makes very heavy demands on the queen: she has to eat enough both for herself and for her litter, which together can soon weigh as much as she does.

When the kittens are about three to four weeks old, the situation begins to change. They

Horatio Henry COULDERY
The New Arrival (Detail)

are now much more mobile and begin to investigate their surroundings. Their mother takes over the role of teaching them to deal with what they will eat, once weaned. She directs their play behavior toward the predatory skills that will be needed for their survival. In a domestic situation, this will include showing them where the food bowls are set out. Even after weaning, the queen continues the tuition as she takes her kittens on patrol with her. The complex procedures that will be used for the rest of their lives are instilled very rapidly.

Maud D. Heaps
A Persian Cat and her Kittens (Detail)

Henriette Ronner-Knip
Study of Cats and Kittens (Detail)

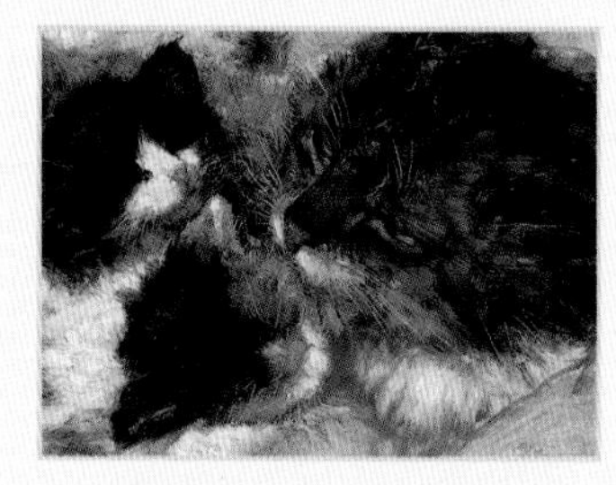

The situtation with big wildcats is very similar. The lion and tiger carry their offspring for three or four weeks longer than smaller species. Cubs are born without any active sense of smell or hearing. As

William Henry Hamilton TROOD
Women's Rights—A Meeting (Detail)

they grow, they begin to explore their surroundings and are trained in hunting skills, just like other members of the cat family. Lion cubs usually take six to seven months to develop enough hunting technique to be of any real value to the pride.

The timeless appeal of mother and young attracts artists of practically every style. When the mother is anchored to the place of rearing her kittens, it makes it easy to complete the work. Equally, the early stages of growth are restricted to the nest area. However, the more active stages—during which the kittens are tumbling around as well as being schooled for adulthood and when the mother has to feed both herself and her litter—present much greater problems for the artist.

Rosa BONHEUR
The Lion at Home (Detail)

GIOTTO

LION WITH HIS CUBS *(Detail)*

[c. 1305]

This is an unusual scene from the Arena Chapel fresco at Padua by Giotto, the master of the medium. It shows a male lion greeting his offspring. In the wild, male lions have very little to do with the rearing of cubs. Eventually young males will become a threat to the leader of the pride; they may even kill the young of a deposed leader. Although Giotto's greatness was his adoption of a more realistic painting style, this lion has a distinctly human look.

Giotto di Bondone [c. 1266–1337]

KUHNERT

A LIONESS AND HER CUBS

[late 19th Century]

The cubs in this painting are very young. Their youth is indicated by distinctive markings: stripes, rings, and rosettes. Most of these fade into indistinction by the time the cubs are weaned, and disappear altogether as they approach adulthood.

Wilhelm Kuhnert [1865–1926]

BERTUCH

THE LIONESS AND HER YOUNG

[1810]

This copperplate engraving was made for a children's picture book. It shows the lion family in the zoo in Paris. The local zoo is still the only place most of us can visit frequently to see lions and other big cats in the flesh.

Carl Bertuch [19th Century]

COULDERY

PLAYING WITH MOTHER *(Detail)*

[19th Century]

The demanding work of raising a litter can become tiresome, particularly when the kittens reach their boisterous "teenage years." The mother cat's tail is frequently used as a toy, but this mother's ears-back signal is a clear indication that enough is enough.

Horatio Henry Couldery [1832–93]

◀ previous page

TROOD

WOMEN'S RIGHTS—A MEETING *(Detail)*

[1885]

This rather satirical portrayal of cats as protofeminists cleverly combines human and feline characteristics. The artist obviously found the idea of female equality a real joke.

William Henry Hamilton Trood [1860–99]

FOTHERBY

BLUE CATS WAKING

[1993]

Some cats just never grow up, particularly if they never leave home. The one on its back is as big as its mother, but is still acting as if it were a tiny kitten.

Lesley Fotherby [b. 1946]

EGYPTIAN

CAT WITH HER KITTEN

[c. 600 BC]

What is so touching about this Egyptian bronze, which is some 2,600 years old, is that it is an everyday portrayal of a lactating queen (notice her swollen teats) with her tiny kitten climbing over her back. Although cats are known to have been part of households in Egypt a thousand years before this, it was in the later Egyptian period that they were deified.

COULDERY

THE NEW ARRIVAL

[19th Century]

There is ambiguity here. Is it the large tabby or the bristling ginger kitten that has just arrived? As usual, Couldery captures the posture, expression, and fur patterns of the cats with great accuracy.

Horatio Henry Couldery
[1832–93]

BURNE-JONES

CAT AND KITTEN

[19th Century]

This watercolor of a cat with her kitten is much more homely than the romantic style for which Burne-Jones is better known.

Sir Edward Coley Burne-Jones
[1,833–98]

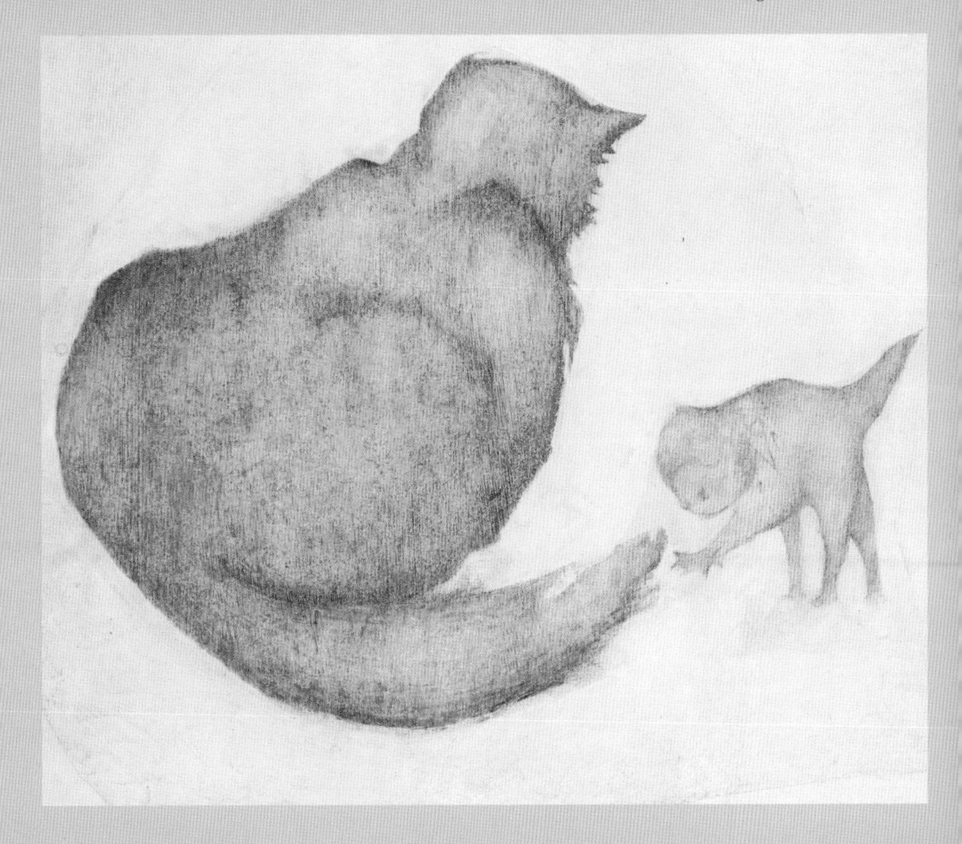

DE SATUR

CATS PLAYING IN A GARDEN *(Detail)*

[1881]

Mother cats encourage their kittens to direct their play toward behavior that will be useful in adult life. Here the kitten's tentative pawing at the blooms is encouraged by the queen. The dignified tomcat under the tree takes no part in this.

Edmund Byrne de Satur [fl. 1878–85]

RONNER-KNIP

STUDY OF CATS AND KITTENS

[1896]

Anyone who has tried to draw or even photograph cats will know that they can prove elusive subjects. Here Ronner-Knip shows extraordinary skill in the style of Thomas Gainsborough (1727–88), Théodore Géricault (1791–1824), and Leonardo da Vinci (1452–1519).

Henriette Ronner-Knip
[1821–1909]

HEAPS

A PERSIAN CAT AND HER KITTENS

[c. 1914]

Somewhat more contrived than Ronner-Knip's work, this is still rather appealing. The kittens still have their baby blue eyes.

Maud D. Heaps [fl. 1913–14]

RONNER-KNIP

MAKING MISCHIEF

[19th Century]

These kittens have reached the rebellious stage, stressful for any parent. The mother cat stations herself somewhere she can keep an eye them.

Henriette Ronner-Knip
[1821–1909]

HUBER

WAITING FOR SECONDS *(Detail)*

[19th / 20th Century]

This charming cat family has its own elegant dinner plate, but their reproachful demeanor suggests that the helpings have been less than generous.

Léon Charles Huber
[1858–1928]

GERMAN

STUDY OF CATS *(Detail)*

[18th Century]

This litter is unnervingly well behaved, much better behaved than Ronner-Knip's naughty brood (see page 224)*, although it is shown in a very unstimulating environment. The mother cat has taken the supervisory position, but there are no apparent dangers. Frisky is not the word.*

DONNELLY

A HAPPY FAMILY

[1868]

The kittens are sleeping in a heap after a feed. Although quite chunky, they are very young, probably not more than two weeks old. Their ears are still rounded and far down on their heads. The mother sits between the door (there could be danger) and her brood. All is well in their world, for the moment.

William A. Donnelly [fl. 19th Century]

“He that loves not his wife and children feeds a lioness at home and broods a nest of sorrows.”

MARRIED LOVE
BISHOP JEREMY TAYLOR
(1613–67)

BONHEUR
THE LION AT HOME
[1881]

At home in this case almost certainly means in a menagerie. The portrait is like a Victorian photograph in the family album, with the maned paterfamilias still in attendance. The cubs are quite young, as is shown by their muted markings that will fade away once they are two to three months old.

Rosa Bonheur [1822–99]

pirate cats

Balthus (*Count Balthazar Klossowski de Rola*)
The Cat in the Mediterranean [1949]

There is no equivalent of the human conscience in cats—or in any other nonhuman for that matter. Consequently there is no guilt experienced when cats "steal" what does not "belong" to them, usually food. Being predatory animals, they are geared up to take every advantage of anything presented to them. This opportunism extends to finding a favorable place to rest or hide, which can lead to unexpected dangers. While jumping into the warmth of an open airing cupboard is harmless enough, chimneys and drains, an open washing machine or tumble dryer can be life-threatening. Open windows in high-rise buildings can present similar hazards. A surprisingly large number of cats risk their lives by this route. While most cats survive such falls, they often suffer a broken limb or jaw.

ANONYMOUS
Still Life With Cat and Mouse (Detail)

Joachim WTEWAEL
Charity (Detail)

Most opportunistic behavior relates to food and feeding. The dominant male lion in a pride always eats the prey first and allows the rest of the group access

only after he has had his fill. In groups of domestic cats, the dominant individuals also dominate the eating arrangements. These are not always the same animals each time, and not always the males. The hierarchy in any group of cats is never permanent. As cats age, become ill or suffer injury, their position in society changes —death removes all cats eventually. Ambitious cats will then take advantage of this opportunity and will establish a higher position for themselves if they can. This is especially evident in lion colonies, where a bold young male may challenge the head of the pride.

Louis Eugène LAMBERT
Kittens at a Banquet (Detail)

Those cats that are dependent on humans to feed them become very skillful in manipulating their owners. Affecting behavior that indicates the desire to be fed includes staring mournfully at the food cupboard and

Lucy A. LEAVERS
In a Fix (Detail)

Sophie ANDERSON
An Opportune Moment (Detail)

making slightly pathetic-sounding mewing noises. This is accompanied by running around with the tail elevated and generally getting underfoot.

The cat's ability to move in, seize food, and withdraw very rapidly gives it a strong advantage, which has been observed and recorded accurately by several artists. Sometimes the cat is depicted partly hidden in a still life, notably in the works of Frans Snyders (1579–1657) and Alexandre-François Desportes (1661–1743); at other times it lies in a more obvious position, waiting to take advantage of humans with food. Cats are sometimes seen in conflict with dogs in paintings. The cat usually signals its antagonism in a very threatening way.

Théophile-Alexandre STEINLEN
Sterilized Milk (Detail)

In sharp contrast to the immediate "lightning strike" is the cat's ability to wait its moment. They will stand motionless in wait over a mouse hole or any other promising source for long periods. But when the time for action comes, it will be rapid.

Hieronymus BOSCH
The Garden of Earthly Delights (Detail)

Dutch genre works frequently show cats eating, or taking food away. These are often meant to be reflections of human behavior. This is exemplified in *Sleeping Maid and Her Mistress* by Nicolas Maes (1634–93), in which the maid is neglecting her duties, while her superior gestures in exasperation. A cat has seized the moment and rushed in to grasp a fowl lying in a dish above the maid. The cat has very ugly, and distinctly human, features. It is a clear indication of the need to be ever watchful.

"And you shall have for lunch or tea
whatever fish swim in the sea
And all the cream that's meant for me
—and not a word of thieving!"

THE LOST CAT
E. V. RIEU
(1887–1972)

ANDERSON

AN OPPORTUNE MOMENT

[late 19th Century]

If there is food around, then cats will take it. The child is dozing after a meal and it only takes a moment for the leftovers to be snatched. If disturbed, the cat will pick up a mouthful and make off with it. Note that the ears are pricked up on guard duty.

Sophie Anderson
[1823–1903]

HAYES

TOMORROW WILL BE FRIDAY *(Detail)*

[late 19th Century]

In the Catholic tradition, fish is the ingredient for Friday's meal. On Thursday, therefore, the fish is out, ready to be prepared. The kitten is outnumbered and is letting discretion be the better part of valor.

John Hayes
[fl. 1897–1902]

LAMBERT

KITTENS AT A BANQUET *(Detail)*

[19th Century]

It may look like the party's over, but not for this band of marauding kittens led by their mother; she is teaching them how to take advantage of their human companions.

Louis Eugène Lambert [1825–1900]

“With wide unblinking stare
The cat looked; but she did not see the king.
She only saw a two-legg'd creature there
Who in due time might have tit-bits to fling.”

CATS AND KINGS

ALFRED NOYES

(1880–1958)

ENGLISH

I'LL HAVE YOUR PLUM PUDDING

[c. 1880/90]

Cats have very little ability to taste sweet things, but that will never stop them from hanging around any food source, just in case a savory morsel comes their way. The black cat on this Christmas card is a good-luck symbol, very appropriate for seasonal greetings.

I'LL HAVE YOUR PLUM PUDDING.
A Merry Christmas

FLEMISH

JANUARY: CAT IN A ROOM

[c. 1525]

Although more than 450 years old, this medieval calendar shows how cats and cat behavior have not changed at all. This very well fed, homely cat is far more than just a ratter. It is waiting for something to fall from the table; or for the servant to allow it a sample from the sizeable dish on the table; or, even better, for the servant to leave the room.

ITALIAN
BIRTH OF THE VIRGIN
[c. 1480]

The Virgin's mother, St. Anne, in this painting from the Venetian School, has recovered from the process of giving birth and is more than ready for some food. As it is being provided, the household cat, a robust and very well fed tabby with some tigerlike features, arrives on cue to take what is going, as if by right.

GIACOMETTI
CAT: MAÎTRE D'HÔTEL
[c. 1967]

This amusing bronze is said to be the cat as maître d'hôtel. If it behaves in a typical feline manner, it is more likely to be seeking food than providing it. The artist, Diego Giacometti, was brother, lifelong assistant, and model for the more famous Giacometti, sculptor Alberto (1901–66).

Diego Giacometti
[1902–85]

BONNARD

THE BOWL OF MILK

[1919]

This picture was originally entitled Interior at Antibes. *The glorious Mediterranean light floods into the room, but the cat is in shadow. Bonnard frequently included cats and dogs in his works. They are not always immediately obvious—a nose here, a tail there—but are always worth seeking out.*

Pierre Bonnard [1867–1947]

STEINLEN

STERILIZED MILK

[1904]

In this poster, sterilized milk comes across as the nectar of the gods.The cats seem to think (probably correctly) that they will get their share of the milk by sheer stare power.

Théophile-Alexandre Steinlen [1859–1923]

“ When the tea
is brought in at
five o'clock
And all the
neat curtains are
drawn with care,
The little black
cat with the
bright green eyes
is suddenly
purring there.
The white saucer
like some full
moon descends
At last from the
clouds of the
table above. ”

MILK FOR THE CAT

HAROLD MUNRO

(1879–1932)

WTEWAEL

CHARITY

[1627]

Painted toward the end of the artist's life, this work reflects the more realistic style he eventually adopted. Everybody is being offered food. The dog has allowed itself to be held back; the cat has cunningly got itself into a position within easy reach of the child's bowl.

Joachim Wtewael [1566–1638]

GRYEFF

SERVANT PREPARING VEGETABLES AND GAME OUTSIDE A COTTAGE

[17th / 18th Century]

Amid a plentiful supply of food, the cat has stationed itself between the vegetables and the game. While the servant is distracted by the magpie in the cage, the moment is right for the cat to capture and run off with a small trophy, which lies within easy striking distance.

Adriaen de Gryeff [1645–1718]

BASSANO

THE LAST SUPPER

[16th Century]

Francesco the Younger was one of a large family of artists from Bassano in Italy who specialized in biblical themes that were realized as rustic genre scenes, complete with convincingly peasant-style people and very naturalistic animals. Here the Bassano family cat and dog are included in a version of the most famous meal in Western culture. Clearly unbothered by their proximity to greatness, both pets have taken advantage of some scraps from the table. However, the cat has a distinctly shifty look. This could be a result of the sound of the wine being poured. Alternatively, the cat may be included as a symbol of the treachery of Judas Iscariot.

Bassano (Francesco da Ponte the Younger)
[1549–92]

"Lat take a cat, and
fostre him well with milk,
And tendre flesh, and
make his couch of silk,
And lat him see a mous
go by the wall;
Anon he weyveth milk,
and flesh, and al
And every deyntee
that is in that house
Swich appetyt hath
he to ete a mous..."

THE CANTERBURY TALES
GEOFFREY CHAUCER
(c. 1340–1400)

THE SCOTSMAN

RONNER-KNIP

A BIT OF CHEESE *(Detail)*
[19th Century]

In most households where there are dogs and cats, it is not unusual for the cats to run things. Here is a classic two-handed dummy pass: the mother cat diverts the apprehensive pug dog, valiantly defending an empty dish, while on the table the kitten is making a bid for the cheese.

Henriette Ronner-Knip
[1821–1909]

“Ho, all you cats in all the street;
Look out, it is the hour of meat.”

CAT'S MEAT
HAROLD MUNRO
[1879–1932]

NIELSSEN

RUDI AND THE MISCHIEVOUS TABBIES
[19th Century]

In this picture the dog is having rather more success in policing the table. However, the cats have the advantage of height and have gained their objective. One, possibly the mother, hisses defiance, while the other gets on with raiding the food.

Clemence Nielssen
[fl. 1879–1911]

CHARDIN

THE RAY FISH

[1738]

Food left lying around is a strong temptation to cats of all ages. This kitten has been caught red-handed on a table where there is fish as well as oysters. Its startled reaction is almost certainly a result of stepping on the oyster shells.

Jean-Baptiste Chardin [1699–1779]

LEAVERS

IN A FIX

[19th Century]

Sometimes the plan just doesn't come together. The cat's intention to get at the hen's chicks has been thwarted and there is a standoff, from which no one can escape with dignity.

Lucy A. Leavers [fl. 1887–98]

“ The time and my
intents are savage wild
More fierce and more
inexorable far
Than empty tigers or
the roaring sea. ”

ROMEO AND JULIET
WILLIAM SHAKESPEARE
(1564–1616)

TOWNE

TIGERS IN A WOODED LANDSCAPE

(Detail)

[c. 1800]

This is a very unlikely scene. Tigers are not at all gregarious—they normally come together only at mating time. The remains of a kill may be incidental to the dispute that is about to erupt here.

Charles Towne [1763–1840]

BOSCH

THE GARDEN OF EARTHLY DELIGHTS
(Detail)
[1500]

As part of one of the most extraordinary works in all art, the cat is seen making off with a rat. The posture of a cat with a trophy is unmistakable. Although the scene is of Paradise before the fall from grace, there are clear indications of conflicts to come. As Christ presents Eve to Adam, animals that had lived in harmony start to show savage traits.

Hieronymus Bosch [c. 1450–1516]

FRENCH

CAT AND RAT *(Detail)*
[13th Century]

It is clear from the bestiaries of the thirteenth and fourteenth centuries that the main role of cats was to deal with mice and rats. In fact, the mere presence of cats in the household is usually enough to deter rodent inhabitants. Here a cat is featured in a French book of psalms getting on with its proper work.

“Vengeance I ask and cry,
By way of explanation
On all the whole nation
Of cats wild and tame;
God send them sorrow and shame!
The cat specially
That slew so cruelly
The little pretty sparrow
That I brought up at Carrow.”

A CURSE ON THE CAT
JOHN SKELTON
(c. 1460–1529)

LAMBERT
BEST OF FRIENDS *(Detail)*
[19th Century]

Domestic cats can live in the same environment as many other species, provided there is enough food for all. Here a tame magpie (which is famed for thieving) shares the leftovers from a meal with a kitten. The mother cat stands by, overseeing everything to make sure that her kitten gets its share.

Louis Eugène Lambert [1825–1900]

"He has gone to fish for his Aunt Jobiska's Runcible Cat with crimson whiskers."

THE POBBLE WHO HAS NO TOES
EDWARD LEAR
(1812–88)

PICASSO
CAT AND CRAB ON THE BEACH
[1965]

Most of Picasso's works startle in some way. Although the shapes are far from being merely representational, the bemused cat confronted with a very strange-looking crab is not at all sure what to make of it. The tail is held up in defiance and maybe the fur is bristling. The need to take advantage of every food opportunity cannot override the technical difficulties of an armored crustacean.

Pablo Picasso [1881–1973]

ANONYMOUS

STILL LIFE WITH CAT AND MOUSE

[1820]

Even though this work is of the Primitive School, it shows a well-observed representation of a cat coming across a mouse. The cat's pupils are narrowed, allowing it to focus more accurately but retain enough vision to pounce.

GASSON

THE AFTERNOON NAP

[19th Century]

This enterprising cat has found the remains of someone's meal and a comfortable straw-lined bed to rest and digest in.

Jules Gasson

[fl. 1836–81]

socializing cats

Micha Koeck *Dreams of the Jungle* [***Undated***]

If we tend to see cats as small humans, giving them appropriate names, they probably see us as large cats. They interact with us almost as much as they interact with each other. When we become part of each other's social circle, the relationship can be very rewarding for both parties. We provide food, shelter, care, and attention; they are a source of company, entertainment, and delight. In addition, they deter unwanted invaders, such as rats and mice.

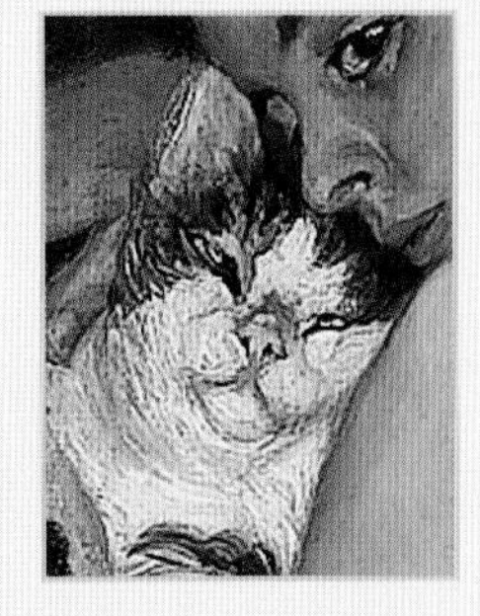

Pierre-Auguste RENOIR
Boy with Cat (Detail)

Cats that are not properly socialized with people before they are a few months old will never fully integrate into human society. Farmyard and other feral-living cats benefit from being fed by humans, but will not normally allow an approach beyond their "flight distance"—an area of about 6–7 feet (2–2.5 meters). If they are caught, they will usually resist handling very fiercely.

Kittens start by learning to live in harmony with their littermates. If they are brought up in isolation, they will not

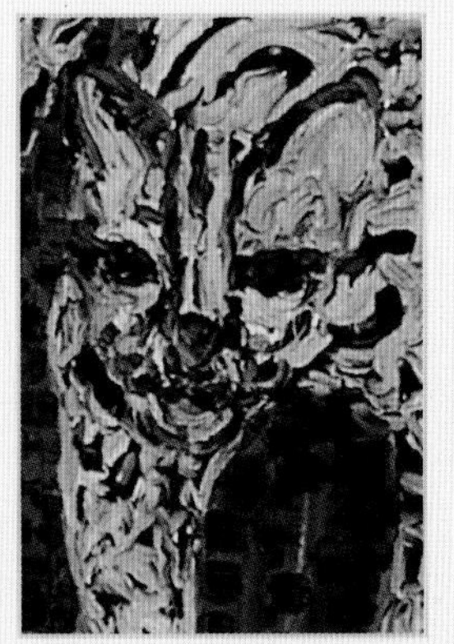

◀ *Hunt* SLONEM
Ocelots (Detail)

be able to relate peacefully to their own species. Socialization with people can be achieved by gentle, regular handling of kittens from an early age. This quiet approach needs to be exercised on every possible occasion, in order to build a lasting bond between cat and companion.

Théophile-Alexandre STEINLEN
The Chéron Veterinary Clinic (Detail)

Julius ADAM
Cats (Detail)

The process of marking objects around the house, by rubbing the secretions from the glands beside the mouth, continues when cats rub against us. The more we encourage cats to mark us in this way, the better we will get along with them. However, great care does need to be taken when touching very sensitive structures, such as their ears, eyes, nose, and whiskers.

Most cats do not respond well to being lifted and carried around, although they can be habituated to being transported in this way, if they feel safe and well supported underneath. Cats do *not* feel safe and relaxed if hugged. One painting by Pierre-Auguste Renoir (1841–1919), *Girl with a Cat* (*see page* 286), exactly captures a cat's unease at languishing in the inexpert clutches of its young mistress.

Almost all fit and well cats enjoy play. They will tumble around with each other, with another animal, or with imaginary objects if they are alone. With humans they will chase a piece of knotted string or a feather. But, just as with "petting," the cat will eventually decide that it has had enough and will go off for a rest somewhere.

Johann ZOFFANY
Portrait of Sophia Dumergue (Detail)

Suzanne VALADON
Louison and Raminov (Detail)

Most wild cats are loners, except for lions, which have their own social interactions in the pride. There are parallels with feral cat colonies, which can form quite large groups if food supplies are reasonably plentiful. Bands of feral cats can often be seen roaming fruitful scavenging territory such as hospital grounds or the restaurant quarter of old cities.

Any newcomer—be it human or animal—into feline society will be scrutinized very carefully and is likely to be challenged with a fierceness in proportion to the perceived threat. This is based on experience and instinct. Cats brought up with other species do not see them as a threat. This can extend to dogs, and even rats and mice.

Pierre-Auguste RENOIR
Girl with a Cat (Detail)

Artists portraying human–cat interactions have a rich source to draw upon. There are countless examples in every style of representational art. Where this relationship is seen to best advantage is in the depiction of cats in close contact with people. At one extreme, a cat being held in an uncomfortable position clearly wants to be somewhere else; but a cat stretched out in a blissful state on its owner's lap can be an indication of pure contentment.

CADORIN

NUDE IN A FLOWER MEADOW

[20th Century]

If gently handled from an early age, kittens grow into people-friendly cats. Although the elevation and direct eye contact shown here are likely to generate unease, the kitten appears to have full confidence in its elegant admirer.

Guido Cadorin [b. 1892, death date unknown]

“They were at play,
she and her cat,
And it was
marvellous to mark
The white paws and
the white hand pat
Each other in the
deepening dark.”

FEMME ET CHATTE
PAUL VERLAINE (1844–96)

Pears
C Burton Barber
1894

BARBER
SUSPENSE
[1894]

This poster is one of many that advertise Pears Soap. The pets are holding back as the child says grace. The dog does so as instructed, the kitten probably because there is little to command its interest in a boiled egg and toast.

Charles Burton Barber [1845–94]

LARSSON
BRITA WITH SUNFLOWERS
[19th Century]

Larsson was a painter and book illustrator, who is best known for his happy domestic scenes painted at the turn of the century. Here his daughter Brita is seen in the garden with her cat, whose love and affection are encouraged by crumbs dropped from his mistress's sandwich.

Carl Larsson [1853–1919]

“Miss Tibbles is
my kitten; white
As day she is and
black as night.”

MISS TIBBLES
IAN SERRAILLIER
(B. 1912)

GAUGUIN

NIGHT CAFÉ AT ARLES

[1888]

It is no coincidence that the little black and white cat hidden under the billiard table reflects the lady's clothing in this scene from Gauguin's period in the South of France. They obviously have an understanding.

Paul Gauguin [1848–1903]

MASTER OF KÖLN

BIRTH OF MARY *(Detail)*

[1485]

This fifteenth-century altarpiece was painted by an artist who was known simply as the "Master of the Life of Mary." The white cat, a symbol of purity, is in a prominent position to the fore, its curiosity drawn to the pouring of water, which leads the eye of the viewer around the painting and back to the newborn child.

Master of Köln [fl. 1460–90]

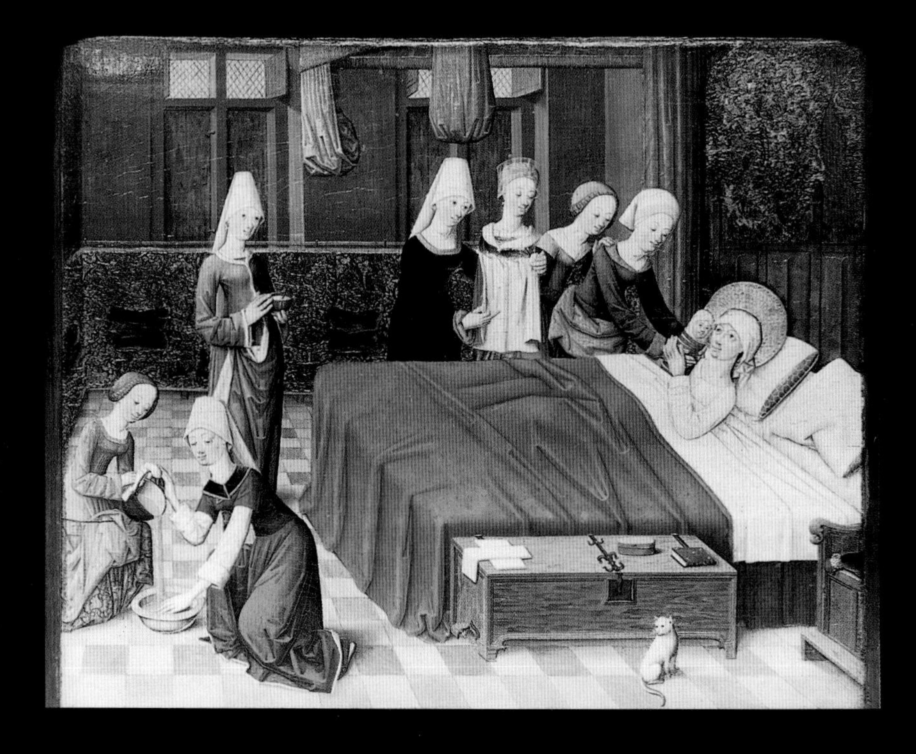

“Look at the gentle savage,
monstrous gentleman
With jungles in his heart,
yet metropolitan
As we shall never be.”

LONDON TOM-CAT
MICHAEL HAMBURGER
(B. 1924)

CAMPOS
DINNERTIME
[1996]

The artist subtitles this work The Antagonist, the Protagonist and the “Cat”alyst. *It is a tense triangle formed by the menacing black dog, the nurturing (about to become peacemaking) woman, and the cool prey—a wide-eyed black cat.*

Theresa Campos [b. 1948]

STEINLEN
CHÉRON
VETERINARY CLINIC POSTER
[1905]

Not only does Steinlen display his cats with his usual skill in this poster advertising a veterinary clinic, but he crystallizes the strength of the interrelationship that we have with our pets—what is known as the Human/Companion Animal Bond.

Théophile-Alexandre Steinlen
[1859–1923]

"They say the Lion and the Lizard keep The Courts where Jamshyd gloried and drank deep".

THE RUBÁIYÁT OF OMAR KHAYYÁM
TRS. EDWARD FITZGERALD
(1809–83)

SCORZA

ORPHEUS ENCHANTS THE ANIMALS *(Detail)*

[17th Century]

Orpheus is playing a viol (lira da braccio), rather than his usual lyre, to pacify all the animals, including two big cats, which would otherwise be having a predatory field day. Note the lion's hypnotized expression. The Maenads (whom Orpheus had angered) approach in the distance, intent on tearing Orpheus to pieces, so the harmonious scene will soon be shattered.

Sinibaldo Scorza [1589–1631]

ROQUEPLAN

THE LION IN LOVE

[1836]

The great lion has fallen under the maiden's spell and is allowing her to remove his sharp claws. This will allow her companions (seen cowering in the background) to pass by unmauled. This illustrates one of the fables written by the French poet Jean de La Fontaine (1621–95).

Camille-Joseph-Étienne Roqueplan [1800–55]

DÜRER

ST. HIERONYMUS (JEROME) IN HIS CELL *(Detail)*

[1514]

Painter and engraver Dürer produced many works of religious significance and numerous images of animals, especially of the exotic type. Here the two are combined in a copperplate engraving. St. Jerome, who translated the Bible from Hebrew into Latin in the fourth century, is said to have removed a thorn from a lion's paw. After this, the lion became the lifelong friend of the saint and the two are often depicted together.

Albrecht Dürer [1471–1528]

“ She holds him tight upon her knee
The graceful animal
And all the people look at him
He is so beautiful ”

THE SINGING CAT
STEVIE SMITH
(FLORENCE MARGARET SMITH)
(1903–71)

VALADON

LOUISON AND RAMINOV

[1920]

Painter, etcher, and printmaker, Suzanne Valadon was the mother of the artist Maurice Utrillo (1883–1955). She had modeled for Edgar Degas (1834–1917) and Pierre-Auguste Renoir (1841–1919), but established herself as an artist in her own right with their encouragement. The enormous, colorful cat chews playfully at the sitter's hand. This is usually a signal that the cat has had enough of being restrained and will soon make an effort to jump down.

Suzanne Valadon [1867–1938]

BOILLY

GABRIELLE ARNAULT AS A CHILD

[c. 1800]

The human sitter is the daughter of Vincent Arnault, who was Secretary of the Académie Française when Boilly was active. The other sitter is an Angora-type with a look of unease, although it appears to be well supported. Perhaps the cat was included to keep the little girl still during portrait sessions. Both stare out of the picture with large, slightly mournful eyes. Cats will usually sit on laps if they feel safe, but only for as long as they want to.

Louis-Léopold Boilly [1761–1845]

FECHNER

THE EVENING

[19th Century]

In this lithograph, the young lady dozes, perhaps after a glittering evening at the theater. She is so tired that she has not even taken off her cloak and bonnet. Her little cat has obviously awaited her return with impatience and is finding the trailing cloak totally fascinating, in the absence of any attention from its mistress.

Éduard Clemens Fechner [1791–1861]

BEAUX

SITA AND SARITA *(Detail)*

[1893–94]

The handsome Sarita is Mrs. Walter Turle (née Sarah Leavitt) of Philadelphia, the artist's mother. The blazing-eyed Sita is her affectionate cat, seen in a pose that is similar to, but more tranquil than, the black cat in Édouard Manet's Olympia (1863).

Cecilia Beaux [1863–1942]

RENOIR

GIRL WITH A CAT

[1875]

Renoir painted a number of portraits of young ladies holding cats. This cat looks particularly anxious because it is being kept in an uncomfortable position. It is supported from below, but it would be much more relaxed in a horizontal attitude. Compare the artist's Julie Manet with Cat (see page 78)*, in which the cat is completely at ease in a much happier position.*

Pierre-Auguste Renoir [1841–1919]

ADAM

CATS *(Detail)*

[19th Century]

These are obviously working cats, employed in a great household (note the old carpet, once a piece of great quality). Perhaps they are a limited company of mother and daughter, mousers by appointment? Their living quarters are neatly laid out, suggesting that, although they appear to be in the cellar, they are well cared for and well fed.

Julius Adam [1826–74]

◀ previous page

RIVIÈRE

ON THE BANK OF AN AFRICAN RIVER *(Detail)*

[1918]

Although the artist was known to have made many sketches of animals in the zoo, this scene, painted toward the end of his life, shows lions in their proper environment and their normal social group. There is no hint of sentimentality as an enormous male patrols the riverbank with the lionesses of the pride.

Briton Rivière

[1840–1920]

ARABIC

THE JUDGEMENT ON DIMNA *(Detail)*

[c. 1350]

In this illustration from an Arabic book, the leopard passes judgement over a group of animals. The species appear to mingle without enmity: their attention is fixed on the judge.

ITALIAN

NOAH RELEASING ANIMALS FROM THE ARK

[13th Century]

This scene is a detail from a mosaic, the Story of the Flood, *one of many at St. Mark's Basilica in Venice. The artist had almost certainly seen very few (if any) lions: both individuals are maned—that is, they are both males.*

دمنة

A BREED APART

I know of no nobler animal. We house cats know our business; we know what we want; we know how to keep our dignity, self-respect, and freedom. No inconsequent, unnecessary running around like a stupid dog. No! We move only when it is absolutely necessary, and then with poise, elegance, balance, with our tails up in the air. No barking for us, no, madam, we know when and how to use our voices. Above all, no licking man's hand; we know better than that.

MARIUS THE CAT (AKA H.E. MARIO GIBSON BARBOZA, ONE-TIME BRAZILIAN AMBASSADOR TO THE COURT OF ST. JAMES'S), *on being asked to choose an animal for his reincarnation*

SLONEM
OCELOTS
[1993]

Ocelots normally live solitary lives in the jungles of Central and South America. This glorious gathering makes an almost abstract pattern of their coat markings, so that individual animals are lost in the swirl and flow of the colors and shapes.

Hunt Slonem [b. 1951]

ZOFFANY

PORTRAIT OF SOPHIA DUMERGUE

[18th Century]

German-born Zoffany came to England in his twenties and painted wealthy people in their grand houses. He also painted the leading actors of the day. The young actress Sophia Dumergue is shown resplendent in a hat of lace and flowers, with a rather uneasy-looking young cat. The gloved arm firmly clamped around it may well be an indication of its liveliness.

Johann Zoffany [1733–1810]

TOULOUSE-LAUTREC

MAY BELFORT POSTER

[1895]

This lithograph was produced as a poster for the Irish singer's performance at the Petit Casino in Paris in 1895. Belfort sang nursery rhymes and slightly risqué songs in English. The climax of her act involved the tiny cat in the song "Daddy wouldn't buy me a bow-wow." It finished with the words, "I've got a little cat and I'm very fond of that, but I'd rather have a bow-wow-wow."

Henri de Toulouse-Lautrec [1864–1901]

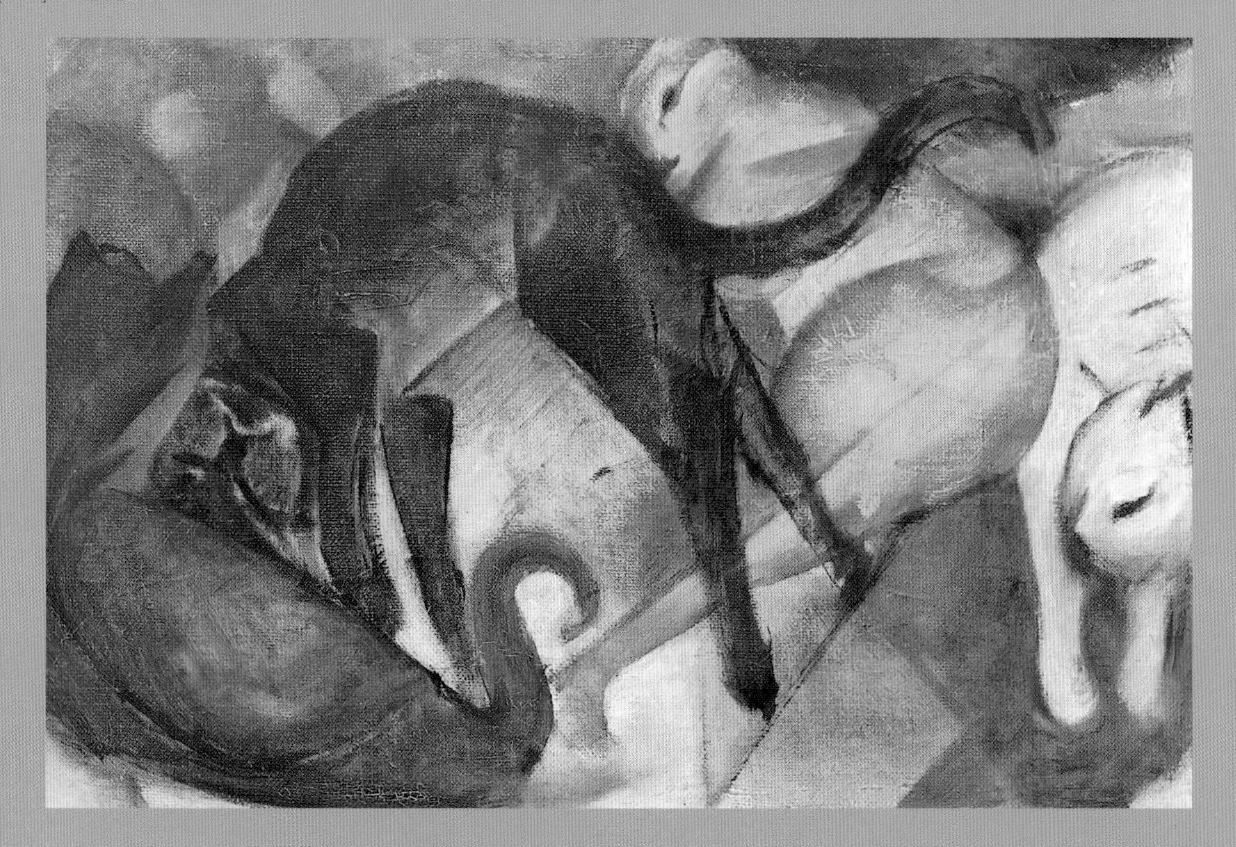

MARC

FOUR CATS AT PLAY

[1913]

In his tragically short life, Expressionist artist Franz Marc painted numerous animals, many of which were cats. In this work they play happily together and form a pattern that has movement, although it is not far away from being an abstract design. Marc was killed in the trenches of World War I in 1916.

Franz Marc [1880–1916]

PICASSO

WOMAN AND CAT

[1964]

Although all thoughts of anatomical precision are a long way from this extraordinary representation of a cat and a woman, all the essential elements are there, even down to the extent of the cat's surprised look.

Pablo Picasso [1881–1973]

"For he is an instrument for the children to practice benevolence upon."

MY CAT JEOFFRY
CHRISTOPHER SMART
(1722–71)

ENGLISH

GIRL WITH KITTENS *(Detail)*

[19th Century]

The pretty child and the attractive kitten have always made a best-selling combination, as can be seen in this heart-melting postcard; but kittens are uneasy about being held off the ground at such a young age.

ELSEY

OUT OF REACH *(Detail)*

[1908]

Children do not always realize the sensitivities of animals such as young kittens, which they sometimes treat as animated toys. Although it is all fun for the puppies and the child, the little kitten is in a very precarious position and it is bristling its fur in a defense mechanism. The work dates from the early twentieth century, a time when pet animals were beginning to be seen as an essential part of the family.

Arthur John Elsey

[b. 1861, Death Date Unknown]

ALLINGHAM

THE GARDEN GATE *(Detail)*

[19th / 20th Century]

The cats in this house are obviously well integrated with their human companions. Mother cat dozes peacefully in the doorway, while the young mistress of the cottage plays with the relaxed kitten. The scene is typical of Helen Allingham's work. She painted cottages mainly in the south of England.

Helen Allingham [1848–1926]

WARD

COMPANION *(Detail)*

[1889]

Ward painted at the same time as the celebrated Neoclassicist Lawrence Alma-Tadema (1836–1912), and his work exhibits some of the same obsessions: marble stone, classical figures, intricate draperies, and a vague feeling of allegory overlaying the scene. The companion here is a tiny black kitten, probably about two months old.

Alfred Ward [fl. 1873–1927]

FRITZ

BAD LITTLE GIRL

[1997]

Fritz is an artist and ceramist who is particularly influenced by Japanese techniques and the fusion between East and West. He works with images from the 1950s that resonate with both innocence and malevolence. This is definitely a classic lesson in how not to behave with a cat. The tail is very sensitive and here the cat is obviously in pain.

Don Fritz [b. 1950]

DEL TORRE

TWO CHILDREN PLAYING WITH CATS

[1891]

Two ways to play with your pet: The older child allows the kitten to sit happily on her lap; the younger child grasps the other kitten to show it off to the artist. This kitten is obviously very uncomfortable being gripped without any support underneath. Children take a while to learn how to play kindly with their cats, but lessons in benevolence should begin early.

Giulio del Torre [1856–1932]

" O lovely Pussy!
O Pussy my love,
What a beautiful Pussy
you are,
You are,
You are!
What a beautiful
Pussy you are! "

THE OWL AND THE PUSSY CAT
EDWARD LEAR
(1812–88)

MASSARD

LADY WITH CAT

[19th / 20th Century]

In homage to the outstanding society portraitist of the Edwardian era, John Singer Sargent (1856–1925), a very elegant lady rests in comfort with her pet cat. It is difficult to see where the cat begins and the lady ends, but note the parallel position of the eyes; cat and lady share some profound secrets.

Charles Massard [1871–1913]

RENOIR

BOY WITH CAT

[1868]

Most of Renoir's nudes are women. Unusually, this shows a young boy tenderly holding a very relaxed cat. It clearly has complete confidence in its human companion, as it is dozing off in his embrace.

Pierre-Auguste Renoir [1841–1919]

“In the clear gold of sunlight,
stretching their backs,
White as snow see
the voluptuous cats,
Closing eyes jealous
of their inner glooms
Slumbering in the tepid warmth
of their illuminated fur.”

WHITE CATS
PAUL VALÉRY
(1871–1945)

KAUS

THE LEGEND OF THE WOMAN WITH A CAT
[1923]

This cat is completely confident in its companion and knows it is allowed to sleep on the bed. Note its very relaxed pose.

Max Kaus [1891–1977]

FOUJITA

SELF-PORTRAIT
[1926]

The Japanese artist Foujita lived most of his life in Paris. He was surrounded by cats, which he immortalized in watercolor with pen and black ink.

Tsuguharu Foujita
[1886–1968]

HODGE THE CAT

I shall never forget the indulgence with which he treated Hodge, his cat: for whom he himself used to go out and buy oysters, lest the servants having that trouble should take a dislike to the poor creature... I recollect him one day scrambling up Dr. Johnson's breast, apparently with much satisfaction, while my friend smiling and half-whistling, rubbed down his back, and pulled him by the tail; and when I observed he was a fine cat, saying: "Why yes, Sir, but I have had cats whom I have liked better than this"; and then, as if perceiving Hodge to be out of countenance, adding, "But he is a very fine cat, a very fine cat indeed."

LIFE OF SAMUEL JOHNSON
JAMES BOSWELL
(1740–95)

HARRIS
PAW
[20th Century]

Cats do not easily "give a paw" or "shake hands," as dogs do. They would normally feel trapped if held in this way. Perhaps this image refers to the hand of St. Jerome tending the wounded lion, or carries the wider symbolism of the socialization of the beast in humanity.

Darren Harris [b. 1972]

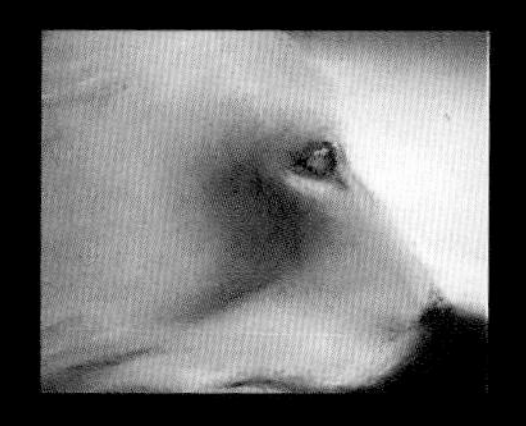

wild cats

Robin PALANKER *Object History (Chair) [1998]*

Gottfried MINDT
A Cat in a Cage (Detail)

It is easy for us to imagine the lion in our fireside cat, or even kittenish activity in cubs in the wild. Many of the characteristics of domestic cats are very evident in the many wild feline species. Even the massive tiger has playful moments, as shown by artists such as Eugène Delacroix (1798–1863) and Trevor Boyer (b. 1948). Most artists, even up until recent times, have had little firsthand experience of big cats except in zoos or circuses. However, the power and mystery of the wildcat can be seen in a large number of works by painters of all kinds.

There are more than 30 wild species in the cat family. They range from the very large lions and tigers to the much smaller wildcat, *Felis sylvestris*, which is a different species from the domestic cat, although it looks very similar and crossbreeding can occur. In addition, there are many types of domestic cat that live wild—that is, they live a self-supporting life, quite independent of human care.

Henri ROUSSEAU
The Lion Hunt (Detail)

The wild species all rest for long periods, stalk and ambush their prey, and then pounce, immobilize, and kill. There are differences in lifestyle, however. Lions are the only wildcats that hunt as a social group. Quite large prey can be brought down by their combined efforts. Although the lionesses do all the hunting, the kill is shared by the whole pride. The males' role is to guard the pride and mate with the females. They mark out their territory by spraying and by the deposition of dung, and defend the group by a good deal of roaring and threatening body language.

GERMAN
Aeros Circus (Detail)

Horatio Henry
COULDERY
Two Cats (Detail)

Leopards, jaguars, and cheetahs look similar, but cheetahs spend their lives in an open, fairly inhospitable environment, while leopards and jaguars live in forest areas with plenty of cover. They rest in trees and remain patient for long periods awaiting their prey. Cheetahs, on the other hand, are geared to outrun their prey, moving faster than any other mammal.

Forest-dwelling tigers are the largest of the entire cat family. Theirs is very much a lone operation—they mix with other tigers only to mate and rear their young. They use their massive forepaws to knock their prey to the ground before employing their teeth to kill it. Unlike most cats, they will take to shallow water.

Trevor Boyer
Tiger Rolling (Detail)

Some of the smaller wildcats become very adept at bringing down the odd bird in flight. Others are able to scoop small fish out of the water with one stroke of their paw.

Shõjõ Kyõsai
True Picture of a Wild Tiger, Never Seen From Olden Times Until Now (Detail)

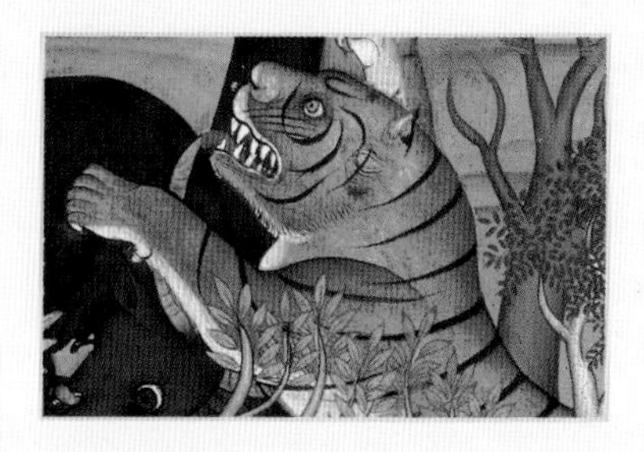

Raja Umed Singh of Kotah
Shooting Tigers, Kotah, Rajasthan (Detail)

Many artists have included animals such as lions and tigers in exotic scenes—usually portrayed in the jungle or other settings with heavy vegetation. Occasionally, wildcats are shown in captivity. Animals such as cheetahs have been portrayed as pet animals on a leash, while the circus provides a subject in which the animals are fierce-looking but remain under human control.

Alexandre-François Desportes
Dog Defending his Game (Detail)

Occasionally, even the most pampered and domesticated of cats transforms into a miniature tiger; this may happen when the cat has been frightened, teased, or threatened by humans or another animal. There are few instances of this in art, but the cat-and-dog fight shown in *Dog Defending His Game* by Alexandre-François Desportes (1661–1743) (*see pages 320–21*) shows that the wildness is only the flick of a claw away.

GOZZOLI

JOURNEY OF THE MAGI *(Detail)*
[c. 1460]

The leopard shown straining at the leash is taken from a cycle of paintings in the Palazzo Medici-Riccardi in Florence. The color suggests that it might be a snow leopard, but it is somewhat too tall and thin for that. It is possible that it was drawn from a description, with the help of a skin used for the fur trade. This individual is being restrained rather severely. It has an ornate collar with lettering to signify its owner.

Benozzo di Lese di Sandro Gozzoli
[1420–97]

FRENCH

HISTORY OF MARCO POLO, ASIAN EXPLORER *(Detail)*
[1375]

Whether or not Marco Polo made his famous excursions to the Far East, his exploits seized the imagination of the early illustrated book market. This comes from a French Book of Marvels, *and Polo and his team look somewhat worried about a trio of smirking lions; the text mentions* animal *sacrifices. But Polo's safety seems threatened here…*

DELACROIX

THE LION HUNT

(Detail) [1854]

Delacroix was the leader of the Romantic school of painting in France, a lover of the exotic, and a master colorist. This vibrant painting is a sketch for a colorful portrayal of a lion hunt for the Universal Exhibition of 1855 in Paris. The final work was severely damaged by fire, but this sketch gives a strong impression of its energy and movement.

Eugène Delacroix [1798–1863]

ROMAN

LION EATING A MAN

[11th Century]

In Rome's heyday, when bread and circuses ruled, Christians were regularly thrown to the lions to entertain the crowd. By medieval times, however, lions had changed sides and were seen as guardians of the faithful. This lion is comprehensively devouring a sinner. It was believed that the male lion never closed its eyes.

“He twists and
crouches and capers
And bares his
curbed sharp claws,
And he sings to
the stars of the
jungle nights,
Ere cities were,
or laws.”

THE TOMCAT
DON MARQUIS
(1878–1937)

DESPORTES

DOG DEFENDING HIS GAME

(Detail)

[1715]

Desportes was famous for his paintings of dogs, game, and hunting, and worked under the patronage of both Louis XIV (1638–1715) and Louis XV (1710–74). Here the hunt has has been brought into the game larder: the fierce dog defends his territory (and food supplies) from a cat that has unwisely brought her kittens in to see what tidbits they can liberate. The mother fights back fiercely, aiming for the dog's vulnerable eye with her lethal claws. It can only be hoped that human intervention will save all parties.

Alexandre-François Desportes [1661–1743]

GERMAN

AEROS CIRCUS POSTER

[1985] *(Detail)*

This very striking poster for a German circus gives a victim's-eye view of a tiger attack. It goes one stage beyond the advertisement for the Zirkus Berolina (see page 32)*; here the wild beast is up close and very dramatic.*

JUBB

OLD TOWN JUNGLE *(Detail)*

[1995]

Is this a ferocious miniature tiger among the houseplants or a full-sized jungle beast improbably transplanted to a giant's dollhouse? Regardless of scale, the stripes and foliage convey the essence of tigerdom.

Kendahl Jan Jubb [b. 1957]

GREEK

° DIONYSUS RIDING A LEOPARD

[C. AD 180]

Wild animals of all kinds, particularly leopards, are associated with Dionysus, the Greek god of wine, as are altered states, and excess of all kinds. In this mosaic from the House of Masks in Delos, Greece, Dionysus's trademark vine-leaf motif can be seen around the leopard's collar.

POLOS

WHEN THE STARS THREW DOWN THEIR SPEARS
[1997]

This is one of a series of five paintings entitled Tyger: New Drawings, *each of which interprets a stanza from the poem* The Tyger *by William Blake (1757–1827). This one accompanies the fifth stanza. One human body-feature is incorporated in each paintng and the series culminates in the portrayal of God as a complete human body with a tiger's face.*

Iris Polos [20th Century]

INDIAN

RAJA GOMAN SINGH OF KOTAH SHOOTING LIONS *(Detail)*

[1778]

The Raja in question ruled from 1766 to 1771 (this is a posthumous study) and spent much of his time on the royal hunt for big cats. Here he has bagged a rather bald-maned lion.

KYŌSAI

TRUE PICTURE OF A WILD TIGER, NEVER SEEN FROM OLDEN TIMES UNTIL NOW

[19th Century]

Kyōsai was a painter and woodblock artist who flourished at the end of the Edo period in Japan. His works are largely satires on the political events of the time. He illustrated Japanese legends and often showed opposing forces as "Beauty and the Beast" or hunter and prey.

Shōjō Kyōsai [1821–89]

“There was a
young lady of Riga
Who rode with a
smile on a tiger
They returned
from the ride
With the lady inside
And the smile on the
face of the tiger.”

ANONYMOUS

“Malevolent, bony, brindled
Tiger and devil and bard,
His eyes are coals from the
middle of Hell
And his heart is black and hard.”

THE TOMCAT
DON MARQUIS
(1878–1937)

SINGH OF KOTAH

SHOOTING TIGERS, KOTAH, RAJASTHAN *(Detail)*
[c. 1790]

The tigers here have been lured into a night-time ambush by a tethered goat. The chances of finding a pair of tigers in the wild were never great, except at times of mating, so it is possible that this scene took place in a hunting enclosure, where the beasts were corralled ready to be picked off by nobles and dignitaries. It is more likely that it was painted as a result of tales told by hunters at the time.

Raja Umed Singh of Kotah [1771–1819]

BOYER

TIGER ROLLING *(Detail)*

[1997]

However fearsome the powerful tiger is, it can still be a kitten at heart. This watercolor is by a contemporary English artist who specialized for many years in painting birds, but has recently turned to mammals, particularly cats.

Trevor Boyer [b. 1948]

HUGGINS

TIGERS

[19th Century]

More noble beasts from the brush of William Huggins (see also pages 138 and 140)*. Here the large male tiger is very well observed, suggesting that the artist was not pursuing it through the jungle. It is very alert and keeps watch over its mate.*

William Huggins [1820–84]

◀ previous page

WARDLE

TIGERS RESTING BY A STREAM

[20th Century]

Although best known for his paintings and drawings of dogs, this artist also produced a large number of representations of many other mammals. Of these, leopards, lions, and tigers featured strongly. Wardle lived near the London Zoo and spent a great deal of his time painting the animals he saw there. The stream shown in the painting is a more temperate zone than the jungle.

Arthur Wardle [1864–1949]

ROUSSEAU

THE LION HUNT

(Detail)

[c. 1900–1907]

The lion is stylized and the ambience is dream-like, but the drama is still very evident in this picture. The lion has pointed ears, like a domestic cat, while lions' ears are rounded.

Henri Rousseau (Le Douanier) [1844–1910]

APPEL

FIGURE AND CAT

[1951]

Here Appel demonstrates his trademarks of violent color and impasto.

Karel Appel [b. 1921]

KIRCHNER
SUNBATHING
[1919]

Many of the German Expressionist Kirchner's works are disturbing, but this colorful scene showing a woman sunbathing with a cat is positive and lively. There are certain echoes of the works of his contemporary Wassily Kandinsky (1866–1944), but this is more accessible. This was painted in Switzerland, where Kirchner had gone in 1917 to recover from a physical and nervous breakdown induced by his army experiences in the First World War.

Ernst Ludwig Kirchner
[1880–1938]

"Minnaloushe creeps through the grass
Alone, important and wise, And lifts to the changing moon
His changing eyes"

THE CAT AND THE MOON
W. B. YEATS
[1865–1939]

HAHN
CAT
[1994]

The Indian brush drawings and watercolors of the Mogul Dynasty (1526–1857) inspired the decorative quality and linear abstractions of this watercolor by a contemporary American artist.

Moira Hahn [b. 1956]

VAN MIERIS

A WOMAN AND A FISH PEDDLER

(Detail) [1713]

The tortoiseshell cat takes no heed of the elaborate relief of the Triumph of Galatea (a sea nymph) displayed along the larder table front. The attraction is in the form of fresh fish, a pheasant, and some duck. The viewer's eye is led from the cat's head to the woman's hands by way of the duck, up to the rabbits, and back down to the cat. The cat gives rhythm and movement to the whole work.

Willem van Mieris [1662–1747]

COULDERY

TWO CATS

[19th Century]

Couldery was the son of a painter, who worked as a cabinetmaker before embarking on a career as an artist. Cats were a recurring topic in his work.

Horatio Henry Couldery [1832–93]

MINDT

A CAT IN A CAGE

[18th Century]

Known as the "Raphael of cats," the Swiss artist Mindt painted many representations of his own feline companions. Most were more homely than this. In this picture, the tables are turned: the cat is the victim, rigid with extreme frustration, trapped in its cage while the rats frolic.

Gottfried Mindt

[1768–1814]

BRISTOW

SCOUNDRELS

[19th Century]

It is difficult to see who the scoundrels are here. Did the boys shoot a bird, which the cat tried to steal; so the dog chased the cat up the tree? Or did the cat kill the bird, the dog chase the cat, and the boys plot to shoot the cat? Only the dog's role seems clear.

Edmund Bristow

[1787–1876]

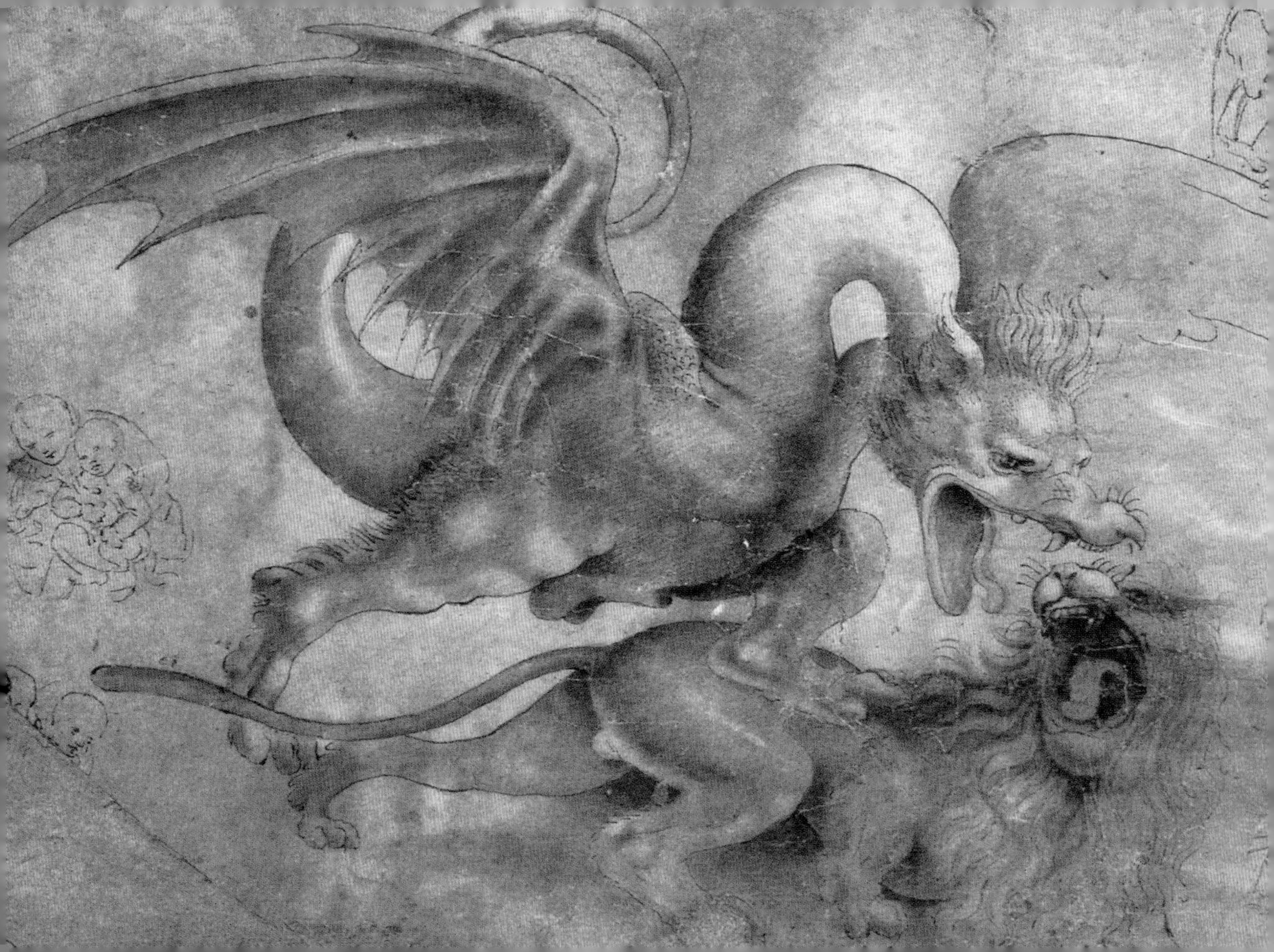

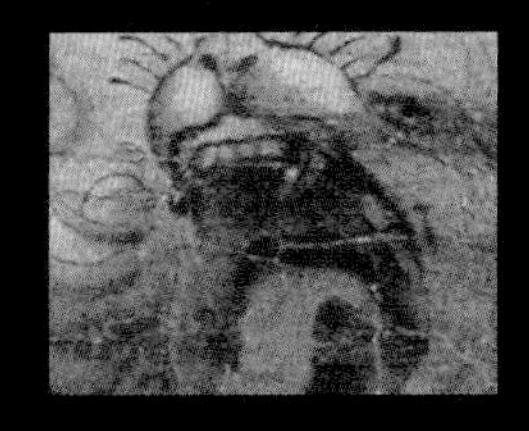

symbolic cats

Leonardo DA VINCI *Fight between a Dragon and a Lion [15th Century]*

Such are the power and mystery of cats that they have generated extremes of opinion for thousands of years. The ancient Egyptians believed that their own souls inhabited cats after death. This led them to protect and worship them, in the form of Bastet, the cat goddess. The opposite view prevailed in medieval Europe, where cats were looked upon by the Church as witches' familiars and were thus considered to be in league with the Devil. The cat's nocturnal behavior—and the startling dilation of its pupil as it hunts in the twilight, along with the reflection of light from its retina in the dark—added to its mystery and to suspicion of it. But the indigenous South American population considered the jaguar to be a sacred beast, its "mirror eyes" believed to be windows onto the spirit world and to have the ability to reflect future events.

◀ *William Bell* SCOTT
Una and the Lion (Detail)

Modern cats mostly live a life of blameless domesticity as part of the family, but they do remain subject of superstitious belief. Some cultures look upon

GERMAN
Coat of Arms of Ludolf von dem Werder (Detail)

black cats as bringers of good luck; others believe they are the harbingers of misfortune; still others use cat representations as a talisman or mascot. In Japan the "beckoning cat," *Maneki-neko*, is considered to be a particularly strong symbol for attracting good fortune.

Feline qualities, such as a strong maternal instinct, have resulted in cats being depicted as symbols of maternity and fertility. Images of the Annunciation, the Nativity, and the Madonna and Child sometimes feature a cat—usually a white one, to indicate purity.

Other qualities are traditionally symbolized by cats: liberty (because cats were believed to be untameable), independence, cleanliness, stealth, courage, and strength all predominate. As cats were believed to be able to see in the dark, they were also thought to be representatives of the Underworld.

Hans THOMA
The Guard at the Garden of Love (Detail)

Donato VENEZIANO
The Lion of St. Mark (Detail)

Human characteristics—such as envy and avarice, as well as lustfulness and general sexual activity—are given to cats in many works. One cat may curl its tail lasciviously around Eve at the time of the Fall; another will be used to indicate Christ's betrayer, Judas Iscariot.

Large wildcats, such as lions, usually represent power and strength and are a favorite choice to symbolize royalty and protection. Stone effigies of lions are used as guardians of a door or gateway. In heraldry, lions in particular are used to denote courage and warlike qualities; they were traditionally so popular that no fewer than 15 different postures were devised to enable them to be shown on a shield.

FRENCH
Bedford Book of Hours (Detail)

Lions have become so associated with certain powerful people that the image of a lion may be used in painting to indicate the person. Haile Selassie (1892–1975), the Emperor of Ethiopia, was known as the "Lion of Judah." The lion is also the insignia of St. Jerome (who is often depicted removing a thorn from the paw of a lame beast) and of the disciple St. Mark. Venice, the city dedicated to St. Mark, has his lion on its coat of arms: a winged lion with a halo, shown resting its great paw on a book of laws.

Edward HICKS
The Peaceable Kingdom
(Detail)

As with the lion, the tiger may symbolize power and military might by its fierceness and strength. In the East, tigers lead a rich emblematic life, representing vitality and animal energy, as well as the god of war. In Chinese tradition, the white tiger is the god of the West, and it is the wind-bringer in the art of *feng shui*. Other cats have their place: traditionally, a brace of leopards drew the carriage of Bacchus, the god of wine; medieval manuscripts were somewhat more down-to-earth, with the cats seen as workers attending to the disposal of rats and mice, rather than carrying heavy symbolic loads.

TIBETAN
Jambhala, Buddhist God of Riches, and his Followers
(Detail)

"Strong is the lion—like a coal
His eyeball—like a bastion's mole
His chest against the foes."

A SONG TO DAVID
CHRISTOPHER SMART
(1722–71)

RIVIÈRE
UNA AND THE LION
[1880]

The Faerie Queen, *written between 1586 and 1596 by the English poet Edmund Spenser (c. 1552–99), is a long allegorical poem in praise of Britain in general and Queen Elizabeth I (1533–1603) in particular. In the poem, the beautiful Una represents the True Religion and her faithful companion, the lion, is England, the guardian of truth. Because there can be no conflict when truth prevails, the lamb can frolic unharmed in the presence of its mighty predator.*

Briton Rivière [1840–1920]

VOS

ORIGINAL SIN IN THE EARTHLY PARADISE

[17th Century]

Consternation in the Garden of Eden, as all the animals look on powerless while Adam and Eve head for the Fall. Things will never be the same again, for the humans will pull the animals down with them. The lions look especially grumpy. The scene is one portrayed by many artists—even the horse looks similar to one seen in the works of Jan Brueghel the Younger (1601–78).

Simon de Vos [1603–76]

HUNT

THE AWAKENING CONSCIENCE

[1853]

Although the cat under the table has a rather evil look, it is "doing the right thing" and releasing the bird from its clutches. This painting is packed with symbols of this kind. The "kept woman" has seen the error of her ways and makes to leave. Her lover does not understand and makes questioning gestures. The moral is that he must let his woman go to a life of virtue.

William Holman Hunt [1827–1910]

BERTIN

DANIEL IN THE LIONS' DEN

[17th / 18th Century]

The Old Testament prophet Daniel was thrown into the lions' den for having disobeyed a religious edict of Darius, King of the Persians. Daniel prayed for deliverance, which was granted; he survived seven days without being savaged. Here the lions investigate the great prophet in an unthreatening manner as he appeals to heaven. This subject was popular with many artists, particularly Peter Paul Rubens (1577–1640), who painted a version in 1615.

Nicolas Bertin [1668–1736]

"The wicked flee where no man pursueth: but the righteous are bold as a lion."

PROVERBS 28:1

SCOTT

UNA AND THE LION

[c. 1860]

This version of Una and the Lion from Spenser's Faerie Queen *has stronger fairy-tale qualities than Briton Rivière's painting* (see pages 348–49). *The lion is more like a giant pet cat than a guardian or predator. The artist was the son of a Scottish engraver, so perhaps he did not want to make the symbol of England too mighty a beast.*

William Bell Scott [1811–90]

THOMA

THE GUARD AT THE GARDEN OF LOVE

[1890]

The garden of love looks more like a sanctuary for naturists, but it is obviously idyllic. The combination of the heavily armed guard and the lion make it impenetrable. The lion, representing strength and vigilance, was often used as a protective symbol at doors and gateways.

Hans Thoma [1839–1924]

NICOLAS OF VERDUN

SAMSON DEFEATS THE LION *(Detail)*

[1181]

It is unusual for such medieval works to be dated accurately and for the artist to be identified. This enamel-on-gilded-copper panel is part of the artist's masterpiece, the altar in the collegiate church of Klosterneuberg, in Austria. There are three rows of panels depicting scenes from the life of Christ and of the Old Testament. Here the text is from Judges 14:5–9. Samson shows his supreme strength and breaks the lion's jaw with his bare hands.

Nicolas of Verdun [fl. 1150–1200]

THRACIAN

HERCULES IN A STRUGGLE WITH A LION

[c. 300 BC]

The story of the first of Hercules' 12 labors has parallels with Samson's struggle. Hercules is shown unclothed, wrestling with the Nemean lion, both personifications of fortitude. As the lion was immune to any weapons, Hercules had to resort to manual force to slay it. Once victorious, Hercules wore its magically armor-plated hide ever after, to protect himself from swords, spears, and arrows.

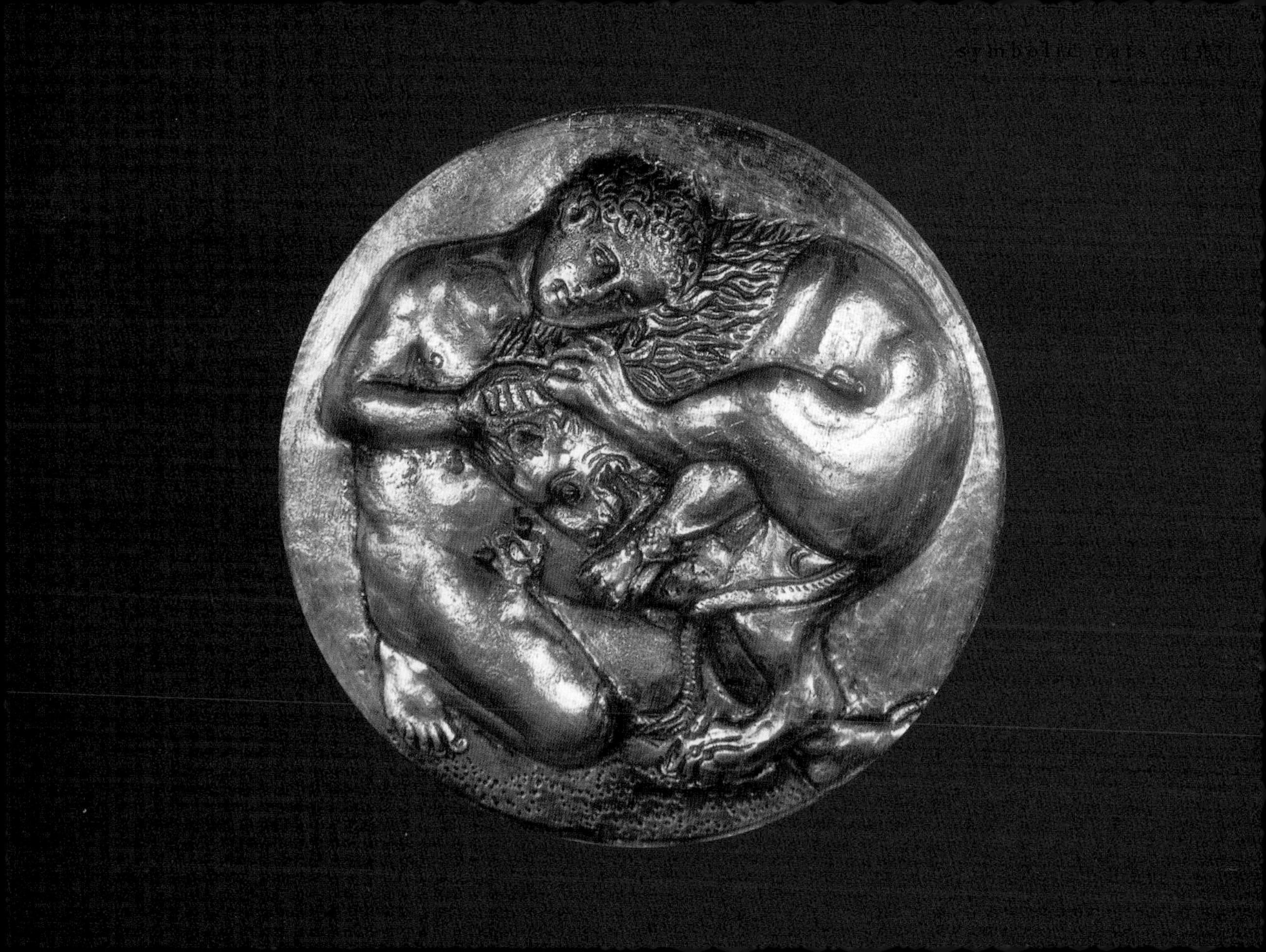

SCHNORR VON CAROLSFELD

SAMSON'S STRUGGLE WITH THE LION

[1860]

The artist had been a member of the Nazarenes, a Protestant group of German artists working in Rome early in the nineteenth century. He worked mainly on biblical and romantic themes. In this woodcut for an illustrated Bible, Samson is seen not attempting to force the lion's jaw open, but in the process of strangling it with his bare arms.

Julius Schnorr von Carolsfeld [1794–1872]

GERMAN

SAMSON TEARS THE LION TO PIECES *(Detail)*

[c. 1360]

Although the subject is the same as that of the painting by Nicolas of Verdun (see page 356)*, the figures here are much more stylized. Samson forces the lion's jaw open and stands astride the animal, holding it in a leg lock. This is an illustration from a book entitled* The Mirror of Human Salvation, *published in Darmstadt, Germany.*

MUSANTE

LION POND

[1995]

The head of a lion forms a water fountain in a park in the Pacific Northwest region of the US, a place that the artist uses as an outdoor studio for painting his signature spiritual, ancient beasts.

Ed Musante [b. 1942]

REICE

ANDROCLES AND THE LION

[1982]

This mixed-media work (gouache and clay on paper) has a theatrical air and a proscenium arch, in recognition of the "religious pantomime" Androcles and the Lion *(1912) by George Bernard Shaw (1856–1950), the Irish dramatist and critic.*

Milo Reice [b. 1952]

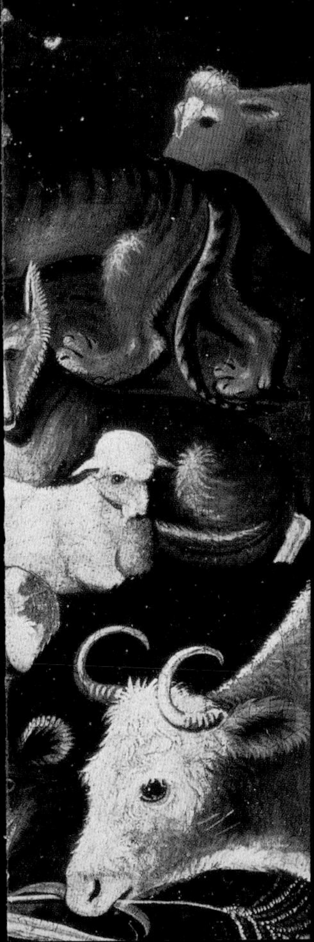

HICKS

THE PEACEABLE KINGDOM

[1833]

Many versions of this engaging subject exist. It is a utopian view of the world, a reflection of the peaceful coexistence as described by the prophet Isaiah, and an echo of the mixed group of animals soothed by Orpheus's lyre. Hicks was a Quaker from Pennsylvania, who painted in the striking style of the "American Primitives." All animals and humans live together in accord, as they did before the Fall from Grace, although the big cats look very wary.

Edward Hicks [1780–1849]

JUDEAN

AMULET FOR THE PROTECTION OF MOTHER AND CHILD

[19th Century]

Lions are seen in their symbolic role as guardians on this amulet, worn to protect the wearer from disease or evil. This watercolour would probably be rolled up and stowed safely in a bracelet or locket so it could be worn at all times.

FRENCH

BEDFORD BOOK OF HOURS *(Detail)*

[c. 1423]

A Book of Hours was a form of illustrated prayer-book-cum-calendar for laypeople. It listed the devotions of the year and illustrated the main activities of each of the 12 months. This example comes from a French version showing a peasant reaping the corn. It has the zodiacal signs for the month, in this case Leo the Lion for the latter half of July and the first half of August.

GERMAN

COAT OF ARMS OF LUDOLF VON DEM WERDER

[c. 1620]

In this coat of arms, the two cats are shown as efficient hunters; each holds a mouse or rat in its mouth. They are probably meant to symbolize the wearer's abilities as a hunter. One cat sits in the middle of stylized grasses. This may be a pun on the bearer's name: the German word for meadow is Weide.

ETRUSCAN

CHIMERA

[5th Century BC]

This is not genetic engineering taken to extremes, but a fabulous beast. It has the head of a lion, the body of a goat, and a serpent for a tail. And it breathed fire. There seems to be a good deal of conflict between the component parts. The chimera laid waste the ancient kingdom of Lycia, until it was slain by the Greek hero Bellerophon, mounted on the winged horse Pegasus.

THOMA

THE WITCH

[1870]

In Western Europe, from around 1400 to the early eighteenth century, cats (especially black ones) were seen as witches' familiars; that is, they were emissaries of the Devil, whom witches were supposed to worship. This color lithograph shows a stereotypical scene.

Hans Thoma [1839–1924]

"The wrath of the lion is the wisdom of God."

THE MARRIAGE OF HEAVEN AND HELL
WILLIAM BLAKE
(1757–1827)

VENEZIANO
THE LION OF ST. MARK
[14th Century]

The winged lion was an attribute of the evangelist St. Mark, who was also the patron saint of Venice. Here he is seen holding a model of his own basilica. The lion is therefore the symbol of the city of Venice. This painting comes from the royal apartments in the Doge's palace.

Donato Veneziano
[fl. 1344–82]

“Be sober, be vigilant;
because your adversary, the
devil, as a roaring lion,
walketh about, seeking
whom he may devour.”

I PETER 5:8

ITALIAN

THE EVANGELIST MARK *(Detail)*

[c. 1480]

St. Mark was said to record the words of St. Peter. In this illustration from the Gospel Book of the Vatican Council *St. Mark is found engrossed in a manuscript on his knees, with his attribute, the winged lion, dozing alongside. Compared with the feline bulk of other depictions of the lion of St. Mark, this beast is smaller and has a very human-looking face. Both have haloes.*

SLONEM

ST. FRANCIS

[1983]

Here is a patron saint for the fauna of the southern hemisphere: this St. Francis is surrounded by parrots, penguins, and playful ocelots, all of which appear to be coexisting in harmony. Slonem's primary subject is tropical birds, and he lives in vast lofts populated with aviaries. But his work ranges from monumental, richly colored masses of birds to sensuous renderings of saints, mysterious figures, and exotic animals.

Hunt Slonem [b. 1951]

BEFORE THE FALL

And God said, "Let the earth bring forth the living creature after his kind, cattle, and creeping things, and beast of the earth after his kind"; and it was so.

And God made the beast of the earth after his kind, and cattle after their kind, and every thing that creepeth upon the earth after his kind; and God saw that it was good.

And God said, "Let us make man in our image, after our likeness: and let them have dominion over the fish of the sea, and over the fowl of the air, and over the cattle, and over all the earth, and over every creeping thing that creepeth upon the earth."

GENESIS 1:24–8

CRANACH THE ELDER

PARADISE

[1530]

All the main happenings in the Garden of Eden are simultaneously shown in this one work. They range from the creation of Adam to the expulsion of Adam and Eve from Paradise. The animals all look a little agitated; the lions are behaving in much the same way as lovers might. The suggestion is that, after the Fall from Grace, the animals' paradise will also be lost forever, through no fault of their own.

Lucas Cranach the Elder [1472–1553]

JANOSOVA
CAVE OF HEALING
[1996]

Janosova often works with archetypes and Jungian concepts. Here a street fighter confronts the female aspect of his personality. The female figure above observes her counterpart—a lioness, powerful but non-threatening, resting in a cave of amethyst, the healing crystal.

Anita Janosova [b. 1951]

“God shield us!—a lion among the ladies is a most dreadful thing; for there is not a more fearful wild-fowl than your lion living.”

A MIDSUMMER NIGHT'S DREAM
WILLIAM SHAKESPEARE
[1564–1616]

CRANACH THE ELDER
THE FALL FROM GRACE
[1533]

One of a number of Cranach's paintings of Adam and Eve, this shows the moment when Eve offers the apple to Adam. Matters are about to change forever in Paradise. The lion, which had lived in peaceful, incurious coexistence with the stag, is about to enter a world of conflict. Cranach shows it waking up to the new power structure and eyeing its potential prey speculatively.

Lucas Cranach the Elder
[1472–1553]

" I seem forsaken and alone
I hear the lion roar
And every door is shut but one
And that is Mercy's door. "

OLNEY HYMNS
WILLIAM COWPER
(1731–1800)

LO SPAGNA
ST. JEROME IN THE DESERT
[1511]

The artist, known as Lo Spagna (the Spaniard), included this panel at the base of an altar dedicated to the "Crowning of the Virgin" in Todi, Italy. St. Jerome was a Christian scholar from Croatia living around the year AD *400. He lived for a number of years as a hermit and penitent (hence the stone, with which to beat his chest) in the Syrian desert. Later he is said to have encountered an injured lion at the gate of his monastery. While the monks fled, Jerome removed a thorn from the lion's paw and tended the wound until it was better. The lion became the saint's devoted friend and is usually portrayed with him as a symbol of solitude, boldness, fortitude, and guardian of the faith.*

Lo Spagna (Giovanni di Pietro Spagna) [c. 1450–1528]

TIBETAN

JAMBHALA, BUDDHIST GOD OF RICHES, AND HIS FOLLOWERS *(Detail)*

[c. 1450]

This is a tangka, *or Buddhist prayer flag. The lion is seen as a symbol of the wisdom of Buddhism and as a defender of its laws. The control over the handheld lion cub signifies the influence of Buddha on the world.*

ENGLISH

MOSES AND AARON

[early 17th Century]

The exquisite needlework on this petit-point book cover (probably for the Old Testament) shows a variety of animals and plants. Moses is depicted holding the tablets and Aaron, his elder brother, a lamp of incense. On the spine are four charming animals: the top one appears from its spots to be a leopard; the bottom one, a rather benign lion, sits as guardian of the faith.

EXOD
THOU
SHAL
FEA
GOD

TURKISH

LION IN A STRUGGLE WITH A DRAGON

[late 16th Century]

The Turkish Empire reached its peak in the sixteenth century, after which it encountered increasing tension with most of the countries of Eastern Europe. It is unusual to find figurative art from this area. This example, showing a lion locked in combat with a dragon, is a book illustration, so it may have been done by a Western artist.

GREEK

MAENAD WITH SNAKES IN HER HAIR

[c. 490 BC]

The Maenads were attendants of the Greek god Bacchus, and took part in the wild ceremonies celebrating the products of the vine. The Maenad on this white-ground vase painting has become so frenzied that she has taken up one of the leopards that draw Bacchus's triumphal car and appears to be beating it with a thyrsus (the massive staff clad with ivy and vine leaves and topped with a pine cone, attributed to Bacchus).

MERLINO

FOR SALE, F15 WITH A TROPICAL HOLIDAY

[1988]

To promote an imaginary used fighter aircraft sale, an ocelot is featured to illustrate an even more imaginary tropical vacation. The ocelot is found only in small numbers in the Americas. It is very rare in North and Central America, but does still survive in South America.

Silvio Merlino [b. 1952]

GIAMBONO

LION IN MAJESTY

[c. 1430]

The ferocious winged lion, the attribute of St. Mark the Savior of Venice, is shown protecting his patron's gospel.

Michele di Taddeo Giambono

[fl. 1420–62]

index of artists

JULIUS ADAM
[1826–74]
PAGES 94, 267, 286–87

HELEN ALLINGHAM
[1848–1926]
English watercolorist and illustrator of Thomas Hardy's novel Far From the Madding Crowd *(1874), she is best known for her paintings of country cottages in the south of England in the second part of the nineteenth century. Children and animals featured prominently in her idyllic settings.*
PAGES 300–301

LAWRENCE ALMA-TADEMA
[1836–1912]
Although born in The Netherlands, Alma-Tadema became a British subject in 1873 and was knighted in 1899. His romanticized versions of life in classical Egypt, Greece, and Rome were decorated with many beautiful women and exotic animals.
PAGES 185–87

SOPHIE ANDERSON
[1823–1903]
French-born genre, landscape, and portrait painter who moved with her family to the United States in 1848. There she married an English artist, Walter Anderson, and they subsequently moved to England, where she exhibited at the Royal Academy from 1855 to 1896.
PAGES 234, 236–37

KAREL APPEL
[b. 1921]
Contemporary Dutch painter and sculptor who helped to found the Reflex group. He is notable for his strident color and the vigorous drawing of his animal elements.
PAGES 334–35

HENDRICK VAN BALEN THE ELDER
[1575–1632]
Flemish artist who painted in the Mannerist style. He was a teacher to Anthony van Dyck (1599–1641), and collaborated with Jan Brueghel the Elder (1568–1625) on both mythological and religious subjects.
PAGES 13, 36–37

BALTHUS [COUNT BALTHAZAR KLOSSOWSKI DE ROLA]
[b. 1908]
Paris-born Polish aristocrat, painter, illustrator, and stage designer. His early works, mainly Parisian scenes, were inspired by the Old Masters and by his friends Pierre Bonnard (1867–1947) and André Derain (1880–1954). After a period of doing erotic paintings and opera stage sets, he returned to his earlier interest, which was landscapes.
PAGES 230–31

CHARLES BURTON BARBER
[1845–94]
English painter who—like Sir Edwin Landseer (1802–73), whose influence is evident in his works—enjoyed the patronage of Queen Victoria.
PAGES 272–73

Théophile-Alexandre STEINLEN
Violet Cat (19th/20th Century)

BASSANO [FRANCESCO DA PONTE THE YOUNGER]
[1549–92]
One of a family of Italian painters, his father was Jacopo Bassano (1510–92) and his grandfather Francesco da Ponte the Elder (1475–1539). He worked mainly in Venice.
PAGES 248–49

JOHN D. BATTEN
[1860–1932]
PAGES 182–83

GEORGE BAXTER
[1804–67]
English watercolor painter and lithographer of historical and sports subjects. He exhibited at the Royal Academy in 1845.
PAGES 72–73

CECILIA BEAUX
[1863–1942]
An American painter, she was born in Philadelphia but completed her training in Paris. She built up a strong reputation as a family portrait artist and completed several paintings of key figures.
PAGES 284–85

ELLEN BERKENBLIT
[b. 1958]
Contemporary American artist who has had several one-woman exhibitions in New York, Vienna, and Chicago and has participated in group exhibitions throughout the US and in Rome. In 1993 she was a recipient of a National Endowment for the Arts fellowship.
PAGES 126, 154

NICOLAS BERTIN
[1668–1736]
French painter in the Rococo style, he traveled in Italy and studied classical painters and sculptors, especially Raphael (1483–1520).
PAGES 352–53

CARL BERTUCH
[19th Century]
PAGES 212–13

ROBERT BISSELL
[b. 1952]
An English-born artist and photographer, now living in Oregon. His whimsical, yet mystical dream images use animals as the narrators interpreting the human world.
PAGE 194

H. BLAIN
[Dates unknown]
PAGES 48–49

LOUIS-LÉOPOLD BOILLY
[1761–1845]
French portrait painter whose scénes galantes brought him into disrepute during the revolution in the late eighteenth century. He is best known for his scenes of everyday life.
PAGE 283

ROSA BONHEUR
[1822–99]
French painter taught by her father Raymond Bonheur (d. 1849). She worked in an academic style and was famous for her detailed and realistic animal portraits.
PAGES 209, 228–29

PIERRE BONNARD
[1867–1947]
French painter of the late Impressionist period whose works were mainly domestic interiors, such as groups around a table at meal-times in the intimiste style. Many are filled with light and include animals, such as cats and dogs, although they are not always immediately evident.
PAGES 244–45

HIERONYMUS BOSCH
[c. 1450–1516]
Dutch painter who created some of the most extraordinary fantasies in art. His works have had a profound effect on art from the Brueghels onward, and still do. Although his allegories had deep religious significance for his times, they also foresaw the surrealist movement of the twentieth century.
PAGES 235, 256–57

TREVOR BOYER
[b. 1948]
Contemporary English painter who has specialized for the past two decades in painting birds, from both life and photography, and has more recently turned to mammals, including the big cats.
PAGES 314, 330–31

EDMUND BRISTOW
[1787–1876]
English painter who specialized in animals, sports scenes, portraits, rustic genre, and landscapes, and was patronized by the Duke of Clarence, later William IV (1765–1837). A recluse by nature, he often refused to sell his pictures and died in obscurity.
PAGE 341

JOAN BROWN
[1938–90]
American artist and member of the Bay Area Figurative Movement of San Francisco. Her works have been included in shows at the Metropolitan Museum in New York, the Hirshhorn Museum in Washington, D.C., and the Oakland Museum in California.
PAGES 128, 135, 176–77

JAN BRUEGHEL THE YOUNGER
[1601–78]
Born into a family of artists from The Netherlands, Jan Brueghel took over the studio after his father's sudden death in 1625. He was appointed Dean of the Antwerp Guild of St. Luke in 1630. The same year he was commissioned by the French court to paint the Adam Cycle. He worked with Rubens (1577–1640) and collaborated with Hendrick van Balen (c. 1575–1632) in creating joint works.
PAGES 13, 36–37

JONATHAN BURKE
[b. 1949]
American artist who lives and works in southern California. He is a magic realist, and his paintings are animated still lifes and revolve around toys, Californian icons, and domestic animals.
PAGES 32–33, 68, 172

EDWARD BURNE-JONES
[1833–98]
English painter and decorative artist (tapestry and stained glass) who was a major force in the second phase of the Pre-Raphaelite movement. Burne-Jones was known for his scenes of classical mythology and medieval legend, influenced by his friend William Morris (1834–96).
PAGE 219

GUIDO CADORIN
[b. 1892, death date unknown]
PAGES 270–71

CRIVELLI CARLO
[c. 1435/40–95]
PAGE 9

THERESA CAMPOS
[b. 1948]
American painter from California who studied with Alexander Calder and Paul Jenkins. Her small watercolors and pastels reflect her preoccupation with home and family.
PAGES 276–77

JEAN-BAPTISTE CHARDIN
[1699–1779]
French painter of still lifes in oil and quiet homely scenes. Later in life he resorted to pastel work because of failing eyesight, but the still lifes, featuring a variety of everyday household objects, that he created at the peak of his career are brilliantly observed.
PAGE 252

FRANZ CHARLET
[1862–1928]
PAGE 38

JUDY CHICAGO
[b. 1939]
American painter, sculptor, and art teacher, Chicago's major achievement was her creation of The Dinner Party *(1974), a work that was regarded as a major statement of feminist art.*
PAGES 52, 80–81, 175

WES CHRISTENSEN
[b. 1949]
American artist and active champion of representative art, his small-scale realistic, watermedia paintings present contemporary models and locations with reference to art history, literature, and mythology.
PAGE 185

HORATIO HENRY COULDERY
[1832–93]
English artist who was himself the son of a painter. He is best known for his paintings of cats and dogs. He was much admired by the critic John Ruskin (1819–1900).
PAGES 89, 91, 96–97, 98, 100–01, 206, 207, 213, 218–19, 313, 338–39

LUCAS CRANACH THE ELDER
[1472–1553]
German painter, etcher, and woodcut artist. He was court painter to the Electors of Saxony and met and painted the religious reformer Martin Luther (1483–1546) in Wittenberg. His works after this became very bright and glossy, with full-length portraits and classical scenes and an abundance of female nudes.
PAGES 372–73, 375

JOSEPH CRAWHALL
[1861–1913]
English painter who was active in Scotland and specialized in animal, bird, and humorous subjects. He gave up oil painting and the plein air *technique in the early 1880s in favor of working from memory, using line and watercolor. Later he developed a distinctive gouache technique using calligraphic brushstrokes combined with high-color accents.*
PAGES 120–21

LOUISA CREED
[b. 1937]
American rag-rug artist, Creed is by profession a flautist and only started making rag rugs about ten years ago, teaching herself how to hook. She

works without a frame, using a latchet hook. Cats and landscapes are the main subjects for her rugs.
PAGES 6, 139

EUGÈNE DELACROIX
[1798–1863]
French painter and lithographer of serious historical subjects, Delacroix was a leading figure in the French Romantic movement. He was in conflict with Jean-Auguste-Dominique Ingres (1780–1867) and was said to have undermined contemporary artistic tradition, yet he still enjoyed official patronage. He disliked progress, yet was forward-thinking in his wish for art to rival the written word.
PAGES 30–31, 108–09, 318–19

ALEXANDRE-FRANÇOIS DESPORTES
[1661–1743]
French painter and tapestry designer, specializing in portraits and hunting scenes. He was part of a movement away from the Italian style toward more of a French ambience, painting directly from nature, as well as the animals in the royal menagerie.
PAGES 107, 315, 320–21

DITZ
[20th Century]
Ditz was born in Vienna, but has lived in England for over twenty-five years. She has shown her pictures at many major exhibitions and is a regular contributor to the Royal Academy Summer Exhibition. Her major passion is the West Coast of America, which she visits twice a year.
PAGE 200

WILLIAM A. DONNELLY
[fl. 19th Century]
PAGES 226–27

ALFRED DUKE
[fl. 1890–1910]
PAGES 169, 197

ALBRECHT DÜRER
[1471–1528]
German painter, printmaker, and writer. He studied under Michael Wolgemut (1434–1519), traveled widely, and set up his own studio in 1497. He specialized in altarpieces that combined painting and sculpture, and also designed woodcut book illustrations.
PAGE 281

ARTHUR JOHN ELSEY
[b. 1861, death date unknown]
PAGE 298

MARTHA MAYER ERLEBACHER
[b. 1937]
American artist and one of the most prominent figurative artists today. Her paintings forgo realism in favor of depicting the inner reality and the moody, sensuous metaphors that bloom from her subjects.
PAGE 201

CHARLES VAN DEN EYCKEN
[1859–1923]
PAGES 40–41, 170, 178

ÉDUARD CLEMENS FECHNER
[1791–1861]
PAGE 285

LESLEY FOTHERBY
[b. 1946]
English artist best known for her paintings of cats. She studied textile design and fashion and is certified as a teacher. Rural farm-life, country gardens—especially where it involves animals—and ballet are further favored subjects.
PAGES 34–35, 127, 148–49, 207, 216–17

Louisa CREED
Murphy (1990)

TSUGUHARU FOUJITA
[1886–1968]
French painter of Japanese birth who graduated from the Tokyo School of Fine Arts then moved to Paris and took French nationality. He was associated with the École de Paris, but still developed his own style. He divided his time between Paris, Japan, and the US.
PAGE 307

JEAN-HONORÉ FRAGONARD
[1732–1806]
French painter in the Rococo style, he was a pupil of Jean-Baptiste Chardin (1699–1779) and François Boucher (1703–70). He worked originally on history painting but progressed to intimate, romantic, and somewhat erotic scenes. His work went out of favor at the time of the French Revolution and he never fully recovered popularity in his lifetime.
PAGES 20–21

FREDRICK FRENCH
[b. 1850, death date unknown]
PAGES 10–11

DON FRITZ
[b. 1950]
Contemporary artist whose work is rooted in the experience of growing up in the 1950s in Germany and the US—a time of both innocence and anxiety about nuclear annihilation. His experiences in Japan have also been important in shaping his current work, particularly his use of raku fired ceramics. One of the cornerstones of his work is the layering of images.
PAGE 302

EDUARD GÄRTNER
[1801–77]
German painter and lithographer, he was the son of a master carpenter. He painted sets for the theater in Berlin and is best known for his urban views and landscapes.
PAGES 42–43

JULES GASSON
[fl. 1836–81]
PAGE 263

HENRI GAUDIER-BRZESKA
[1891–1915]
French sculptor and calligrapher who was killed in the trenches in the First World War at the age of 23. He became involved with the Vorticist movement and worked in London, where he drew animals in the zoo. Although he had a very short life, his work had a strong influence on artists of the 1920s and 1930s.
PAGES 60–61

PAUL GAUGUIN
[1848–1903]
French painter, printmaker, and sculptor who gave up a successful career in stockbroking to follow his artistic tendencies. He became leader of the Pont Aven School and was a dominant speaker in Parisian art circles. He developed his own style, brought about by a hatred of Western society and by inspiration by primitive peoples. He traveled to Martinique and Tahiti, and ended his days in the Marquesas Islands. His work was widely influential on early twentieth-century avant-garde artists.
PAGES 74–75, 274–75

Théophile-Alexandre STEINLEN
Black Cat Poster (1895)

THÉODORE GÉRICAULT
[1791–1824]
French painter born in Rouen and a leading figure in the Romantic movement. He is best known for The Raft of the Medusa *(1819), painted a few years before his tragic death in a riding accident. His work also included many paintings showing other animals in dramatic situations. He painted directly on the canvas.*
PAGES 162–63

ERICH GERLACH
[b. 1909]
PAGES 129, 156–57

JEAN-LÉON GÉRÔME
[1824–1904]
French painter and sculptor who visited North Africa many times in his career. His paintings of Egypt were highly regarded in his time. Later he was seen as a reactionary member of the art establishment.
PAGES 129, 140–41, 168, 183, 194–95

DIEGO GIACOMETTI
[1902–85]
Brother of the Swiss sculptor Alberto (1901–66), Diego seems to have been content to work as assistant and

model for his famous brother, but occasionally turned his hand to small sculptural works of his own.
PAGE 243

MICHELE DI TADDEO GIAMBONO
[fl. 1420–62]
Venetian painter and mosaic artist. One of a family of painters, he also created altarpieces for the churches of Venice.
PAGE 383

GIOTTO DI BONDONE
[c. 1266–1337]
Florentine artist, recognized as the founder of modern painting. He broke away from stereotype Byzantine representation to portray religious figures in a more natural, three-dimensional style.
PAGE 210

BENOZZO DI LESE DI SANDRO GOZZOLI
[1420–97]
Italian painter who was one of the most prolific fresco painters of his time. His capacity to capture current vogues in art ensured that he received a steady stream of commissions.
PAGES 316–17

ADRIAEN DE GRYEFF
[1645–1718]
PAGES 246–47

JOSÉ SOLANA GUTIÉRREZ
[1886–1945]
Spanish painter and writer who was strongly influenced by the writers of the "Generation of 1898" movement. He exhibited widely in Spain and in other countries from the 1920s onward.
PAGES 150–51

MOIRA HAHN
[b. 1956]
American artist living in Los Angeles. Her hard-edged manipulation of watercolor often blends political satire and environmental issues with humor.
PAGE 337

JAMES HAYLLAR
[1829–1920]
Part of a prolific family of English painters: all four of his daughters—Jessica, Edith, Mary, and Kate—were regular exhibitors at the Royal Academy. Hayllar himself turned from portrait painting to popular genre pictures of children in the mid-1860s.
PAGE 26

GAYLEN HANSEN
[b. 1921]
An American painter living and painting in the Pacific Northwest, Hansen concentrates on images of wildlife, such as wolves, bison, cats, dogs, and other creatures. His works are in the naïf style, consistently reaffirming the sovereignty of nature, and have been featured in galleries and museums in the US and Europe.
PAGE 162

DON ED HARDY
[b. 1945]
A southern Californian, Hardy became a professional tattoo artist, developing the fine-art potential of the medium with emphasis on its Asian heritage. He studied in Japan in 1973. Since 1986 he has re-focused on painting, drawing, and printmaking, and has curated exhibitions both for galleries and nonprofit organizations.
PAGE 113

DARREN HARRIS
[b. 1972]
British artist Harris took a degree in fine art, then a postgraduate diploma in painting at the Royal Academy. His work was exhibited in the Royal Academy Summer Show in 1996. He has designed an image for Chevron UK's calendar and his work has also been used as illustration in the Lancet magazine.
PAGES 308–09

JOHN HAYES
[fl. 1897–1902]
PAGE 237

MAUD D. HEAPS
[fl. 1913–14]
PAGES 208, 222–23

RALPH HEDLEY
[1848–1913]
English painter and woodcarver, Hedley was the son of a joiner. He specialized in carvings for churches but is best known for his paintings of everyday life in Tyneside, in northeastern England. Many of his works included the dogs and cats of local inhabitants.
PAGES 52, 63

ARTHUR HEYER
[1872–1931]
Born in Germany, Heyer exhibited in Berlin, then traveled to Hungary.
PAGES 94–95, 154–55, 184–85

EDWARD HICKS
[1780–1849]
American painter raised by a Quaker family, Hicks was a primitive artist of the early nineteenth century. He began as a sign-and-coach painter and became a Quaker minister. He painted farm and religious scenes in oil, with flat colors and simple figures. Approximately 100 versions of his best-known work The Peaceable Kingdom *were created.*
PAGES 347, 362–63

ANDŌ HIROSHIGE
[1797–1858]
Japanese artist born in what is now Tokyo, Hiroshige was the great master of woodblock art. His most celebrated work is a woodblock series Fifty-three Stages of the Tokaido, *a collection of illustrations of the journey from Edo (Tokyo) to Kyoto. Other works include landscapes, as well as homely scenes and illustrations of theatrical characters.*
PAGE 191

DAVID HOCKNEY
[b. 1937]
English painter and printmaker, probably the best-known contemporary artist in Britain, now living in California. His earlier work stressed the male nude, but he now paints landscapes and animal pictures, as well as portraits of friends and family.
PAGES 190–91

WILLIAM HOGARTH
[1697–1764]
English painter and engraver, Hogarth was the son of a London schoolmaster and was apprenticed to a goldsmith. He began painting conversation pieces and moral tales, which were subsequently sold as engravings. His skill as a portrait painter was equally impressive. Public exhibitions of his work enjoyed popularity to such an extent that they led to the foundation of the Royal Academy.
PAGES 118–19

ANTHONY HOLDSWORTH
[b. 1945]
English-born American artist who trained in both England and San Francisco, Holdsworth is highly regarded as an atmospheric colorist who paints on the streets of California, putting a certain urban spin on the termen plein air.
PAGES 64, 145

INDIAN *Lady and a Cobra (detail)* (1605)

LÉON CHARLES HUBER
[1858–1928]
PAGES 225

WILLIAM HUGGINS
[1820–84]
English painter best known for his animal paintings, he exhibited at the Royal Academy from 1846 onward.
PAGES 7, 138–39, 140, 330

WILLIAM HOLMAN HUNT
[1827–1910]
English painter who in 1848 founded the Pre-Raphaelite Brotherhood with Sir John Everett Millais (1829–96) and Dante Gabriel Rossetti (1828–82) His works are crowded with symbolism, combined with a strong feel for authentic backgrounds in his religious works.
PAGE 351

A. JACKSON
[fl. 19th Century]
PAGE 97

WILLY JAMES
[b. 1920]
PAGES 192–93

ANITA JANOSOVA
[b. 1951]
American artist trained in Chicago, Philadelphia, and Italy, Janosova renews the tradition of heroic Old Master narrative painting, producing large, detailed atmospheric paintings that make feminist statements.
PAGES 58, 374–75

PAIZS GOEBEL JENO
[1896–1944]
PAGES 86–87

KENDAHL JAN JUBB
[b. 1957]
American watercolor artist who works in her studio and surroundings in Montana. Animals and birds, both wild and domestic, form her subjects, which are woven into intricate tapestries with Oriental rugs, jardinières, or other patterned spaces to create cloisonné paintings.
PAGES 128, 135–37, 147, 322–23

MAX KAUS
[1891–1977]
German painter, printmaker, and teacher who was born and died in Berlin. He was strongly influenced by Erich Heckel (1883–1970). He was a member of the Freie Sezession and was strongly disapproved of by the Nazis, but managed to survive.
PAGES 306–307

ERNST LUDWIG KIRCHNER
[1880–1938]
German Expressionist painter and woodcut artist, Kirchner was a founder member of Die Brücke (The Bridge), a group of Dresden artists that included Erich Heckel (1883–1970). His best-known works date from his life in pre-1914 Berlin. After contracting tuberculosis he moved to Switzerland, where his decline was accelerated by his works being condemned as degenerate by the Nazis.
PAGES 336-37

GUSTAV KLIMT
[1862–1918]
Austrian painter and draftsman, Klimt was a leading exponent of the Jugendstil movement (German art nouveau). His early erotic paintings caused much controversy, but his later work comprised primarily landscapes and portraiture. He painted Viennese bourgeois women, often against a background of swirls, disks, or geometric patterns. Klimt played an important role in the formation of the Wien Sezession, a radical group of Austrian artists.
PAGES 53, 70–71

MICHA KOECK
[Dates Unknown]
PAGES 181, 264–65

MASTER OF KÖLN
[fl. 1460–90]
In the nineteenth century early artists who had not been identified by name but who could be recognized as individuals were called "Master of their particular subject or their place of work." The Master of Köln carried out work in the churches of Cologne in Germany. He concentrated on painting scenes from the life of the Virgin Mary and so was also known as "Master of the Life of the Virgin."
PAGE 275

WILHELM KUHNERT
[1865–1926]
German painter who trained at the Berlin Academy of Art under Richard Friese (1854–1935). He was one of the first artists to travel to East Africa during the colonial period to paint the wildlife and landscapes of that region. He became known as one of the most important painters of game.
PAGES 210–11

SHŌJŌ KYŌSAI
[1831–89]
Japanese painter and woodblock artist, also known as Kawanabe Kyōsai. He was a pupil of Utagawa Kuniyochi (1797–1861) as a child. His fantastic designs are a combination of traditional designs and drawings from nature, mixed with the more avant-garde. His subjects covered opposing forces, such as beauty and the beast and predator and prey.
PAGES 314, 327

LOUIS EUGÈNE LAMBERT
[1825–1900]
PAGES 233, 238–39, 258–59

CARL LARSSON
[1853–1919]
Swedish painter, engraver, and illustrator. He has a wide range, stretching from massive frescos illustrating Swedish history to domestic scenes.
PAGE 273

Hunt SLONEM
Red Bills (1985)

Kendahl Jan JUBB
Jack's Dragons (1991)

LUCY A. LEAVERS
[fl. 1887–98]
English artist who specialized in painting cats and dogs in a very light-hearted manner.
PAGES 233, 252–53

RICHARD LEES
[b. 1945]
American artist who concentrates on figurative portrait studies. His fascination with the quality of California light is described in his landscape paintings in oil and in his pastels drawn from observation.
PAGE 76

CRAIG LEHMANN
[b. 1953]
American sculptor who works in bronze, Lehmann lives in Colorado, where he concentrates on small-scale depictions of animals and people interacting on a plane of mutual respect.
PAGES 47, 59

JACQUES LEHMANN
[20th Century]
PAGES 204–05

LORD FREDERIC LEIGHTON
[1830–96]
The first British artist to become a peer of the realm. He painted classical scenes, many with draped, seminude female figures luxuriating in exotic surroundings. He benefited from the patronage of Queen Victoria, whose support ensured that he enjoyed considerable success.
PAGES 24–25

LEONARDO DA VINCI
[1452–1519]
Florentine artist of astonishing abilities, Leonardo was one of the key figures in the Italian High Renaissance, producing many of what are now seen as the greatest works of art. Of his many skills, he could capture movement of every fleeting kind, from water swirling in a stream to the activities of cats.
PAGES 342–43

HEINRICH LEUTEMANN
[1824–1905]
PAGES 110–11

JOHN FREDERICK LEWIS
[1805–76]
English painter, etcher, and draftsman born in London. He was a pupil of Sir Thomas Lawrence (1769–1830), under whom he studied the anatomy of both live and dead animals. He traveled widely to paint animal subjects.
PAGES 78–79

JUDITH LEYSTER
[1609–60]
Dutch painter and wife of Jan Miense Molenaer (1610–68). She was a pupil of Frans Hals (c. 1581–1666) and painted genre scenes, portraits, and still lifes in his style.
PAGES 15, 46–47

FRANZ MARC
[1880–1916]
German painter and sculptor, Marc was a leading member of the Blaue Reiter (Blue Rider) Group, which included Wassily Kandinsky (1866–1944), Paul Klee (1879–1940), and August Macke (1887–1914). He is particularly well known for his depictions of animals.
PAGES 50–51, 296–97

JACOB MARIS
[1837–99]
Dutch artist and the best known of a family of brothers who were the leading figures in the Hague School of painting in the nineteenth century. They were influenced by the French Barbizon School, depicting peasant life in a straightforward manner, but were not plein air artists.
PAGE 41

SIMON MARSDEN
[b. 1948]
English photographer.
PAGE 112

JOËL & JEAN MARTEL
[fl. early 20th Century]
PAGE 75

ROBERT BRAITHWAITE MARTINEAU
[1826–69]

English painter and pupil of William Holman Hunt (1827–1910). Martineau was closely associated with the Pre-Raphaelite circle, exhibiting with them on occasion in the mid-nineteenth century.
PAGE 83

CHARLES MASSARD
[1871–1913]
PAGES 304–05

SUSANNA MEIERS
[b. 1949]
American artist equally adept as a painter, costume designer for the theater, and textile designer, or as a curator and editor. Her works are characterized by dream imagery rendered in an operatic manner.
PAGES 177, 203

SILVIO MERLINO
[b. 1952]
Italian artist who creates magical environments where the power of nature collides with man's struggle to control it. Through his work we enter Day-Glo fantasies of a universe where beauty, elegance, and grace are all created through collages that can be described as phantasmagorical.
PAGES 382–83

WILLEM VAN MIERIS
[1662–1747]
Son of Dutch genre painter Franz van Mieris (1635–81), Willem was born in Leiden and continued the family tradition with his brother Jan (1660–90).
PAGE 338

GOTTFRIED MINDT
[1768–1814]
PAGES 4, 312, 340–41

CUENCA MUÑOZ
[fl. early 20th Century]
PAGES 18–19

ED MUSANTE
[b. 1942]
American artist whose oil on panel paintings are intimate homages to wildlife that appears to emerge gradually from ancient times.
PAGES 159, 360

WILLIAM NEWZAM PRIOR NICHOLSON
[1872–1949]
PAGE 5

CLEMENCE NIELSSEN
[fl. 1879–1911]
PAGE 251

JEAN BOE NIESTLE
[fl. 19th Century]
PAGES 88, 116–17

JEAN-BAPTISTE OUDRY
[1686–1755]
French artist and follower of Alexandre Desportes (1661–1743). He worked on designs for the Beauvais, and later for the Gobelin tapestry studios where he was director for ten years. He became court painter to Louis XV, painting landscapes, including the royal hunts; he incorporated hounds in the many still lifes featuring the spoils of the hunt. He is renowned as one of the outstanding animal painters of the 18th century.
PAGES 44–45

ROBIN PALANKER
[b. 1950]
American artist who paints solely with dry pigment, a technique that allows her to explore movement, both of her subjects and of the atoms that comprise all matter. Her other passion, ballet, is used to understand the effects of weightlessness and motion in both her animate and inanimate subjects.
PAGES 164–65, 310–11

FRANK PATON
[1856–1909]
English artist who painted in watercolor and oils. He painted mostly portraits of dogs, usually involved in hunting.
PAGES 158–59

WILHELM PFEIFFER
[19th Century]
PAGES 174–75

PABLO PICASSO
[1881–1973]
Spanish artist who worked in France and dominated twentieth-century European art. Most of his work was in painting, but he was skilled in many other media and had an impact on numerous other disciplines. With Georges Braque (1882–1963), Picasso was responsible for the development of Cubism.
PAGES 2, 260–61, 297

EGYPTIAN *Bastet, Tuterlary Deity of Bubastis, in the Form of a Cat* (6th Century BC)

CHRISTIAN PIERRE
[b. 1962]
American artist who started as a jeweler's studio assistant, then went on to work on various collaborative painting projects in England and the US. In his work he tries to reflect the beauty and simplicity of life as it is and the power we have to change our lives, reminding people to look beyond the surface.
PAGES 124–25, 131

IRIS POLOS
[20th Century]
Contemporary American artist who has exhibited widely in California where she has held various teaching positions and artist residencies. She describes the technique that she uses to create her luminescent images as "painting with pencils." Her works often depict human suffering and spirituality, and draw on a wide range of exotic influences.
PAGES 325

ODILON REDON
[1840–1916]
French artist born in Bordeaux who studied under Gérôme (1824–1904). He first specialized in black-and-white charcoal drawings with a dreamlike melancholy quality. He was highly respected among Parisian intellectual circles. In 1900 he turned to painting, specializing in flowers and portraits in intense colors. He was considered a forerunner of Surrealism.
PAGE 84

MILO REICE
[b. 1952]
American artist whose themes are universal. A master storyteller with a humanist view, Reice never approaches his canvases in a simple way. He takes subjects from history and mythology and reinterprets them in a contemporary fashion. His work is at the same time figurative and abstract, and his constructions are two- or three-dimensional.
PAGES 360–61

REMBRANDT VAN RIJN
[1606–69]
Dutch artist born in Leiden, he moved to Amsterdam where he became the most prominent portrait artist of the time. His series of self-portraits covering the last 40 years of his life are seen as some of the most perceptive self-observations in all of art. He produced a large number of etchings and drawings, mostly of religious subjects, as well as landscapes and animals such as pigs, elephants, and zoo animals.
PAGES 127, 142–43

PIERRE-AUGUSTE RENOIR
[1841–1919]
French painter and leading figure of the Impressionists. Unlike many Impressionists, he made numerous preparatory sketches for his works. His paintings are mainly of subjects where the people are enjoying themselves in light-filled scenes, many of which also include cats and dogs. Many of his works are found in American collections, as he was appreciated here before he was valued in Europe.
PAGES 20, 54, 78, 152–53, 266, 269, 286, 304

BRITON RIVIÈRE
[1840–1920]
British artist who became the most celebrated animal painter of his day. His work with small children and animals could be considered too sentimental for present-day tastes but there is no denying his skill as a draftsman.
PAGES 56–57, 288–90, 348–49

FRANK ROMERO
[b. 1941]
A California native, Romero has been lauded for his artistry and his role as a founder of Los Four, the men who galvanized Hispanic artists and started the Los Angeles Hispanic Art Movement in 1974. His richly colored canvases, painted sculptures, and neon-enhanced depictions of California, and Los Angeles in particular, have been seen in Europe and the United States.
PAGES 130–31

HENRIETTE RONNER-KNIP
[1821–1909]
Dutch painter who was one of a long line of artists in the Knip family that dated back to the seventeenth century. She was born in Amsterdam, married Teico Ronner, and moved to Brussels in 1870. She had a son and daughter who both became artists. After this she devoted her life to painting cats.
PAGES 14, 26–27, 208, 222, 224–25, 250–51

JOHANN HEINRICH ROOS
[1631–85]
German painter and etcher who was a pupil of Karel Dujardin (1622–78)

of Amsterdam. He worked as a court painter in Heidelberg and concentrated mainly on Italianate landscapes and portraits, which included many animals.
PAGE 100

CAMILLE-JOSEPH-ÉTIENNE ROQUEPLAN
[1800–55]
French painter and lithographer, whose work primarily consisted of landscapes, marine and historical subjects, and genre scenes in oils and watercolors. His large-scale anecdotal paintings in the mid-1830s brought him considerable fame, and he made a notable contribution to the regeneration of landscape painting in France.
PAGE 280

HENRI ROUSSEAU (LE DOUANIER)
[1844–1910]
French painter and leading figure of the Naïve artists. He worked as a minor tollgate official (hence the nickname "Le Douanier," the customs man) but retired and, although he had no formal training, took up painting full time in his forties. His highly colored works have a dreamlike quality created by using fantastic backgrounds from enlarged versions of plants from the botanical gardens. Although recognized by Picasso (1881–1973), he was seen as something of a joke by critics of the time. Now his paintings are found in many of the large museums of the world.
PAGES 19, 92–93, 104–105, 188–89, 312, 334

JULES LE ROY
[1833–65]
PAGE 172–73

PETER PAUL RUBENS
[1577–1640]
Flemish painter and diplomat, Rubens was employed as an ambassador by the rulers of the southern Netherlands and became a painter to the European courts. He turned his wide knowledge of classical art and literature into magnificent altarpieces, historical scenes, landscapes, and portraits.
PAGES 88, 114–15

CARL BORROMAUS ANDREAS RUTHART
[c. 1630–1703]
Born the son of a count in Danzig, in what is now Poland, Ruthart traveled to Rome, Venice, and Vienna. He painted animals hunting, fighting, and resting, and was especially skillful in portraying movement. Later he concentrated on altarpieces and other religious works, eventually becoming a Cistercian monk.
PAGE 123

SARAHIDE
[1807–78]
PAGES 90, 102–03

EDMUND BYRNE DE SATUR
[fl. 1878–85]
London painter of domestic scenes, he exhibited at the Royal Academy in 1878–85, and elsewhere.
PAGES 220–21

ANDREA SCACCIATI THE ELDER
[1642–1704]
PAGE 161

JULIUS SCHNORR VON CAROLSFELD
[1794–1872]
German painter and illustrator, he was one of the Nazarenes working on biblical themes in frescos in Rome and Munich. He became the director of the Dresden Gallery.
PAGES 358–59

SINIBALDO SCORZA
[1589–1631]
Italian painter, etcher, and draftsman, he was inspired by themes that permitted the representation of all kinds of animals. He painted nine or ten versions of his favorite subject, Orpheus charming the animals with his music, using painstakingly detailed technique and realistic rendering of both surface and texture.
PAGES 278–79

Don Ed HARDY
Tattoo Royale (1995)

WILLIAM BELL SCOTT
[1811–90]
Scottish painter and poet, son of an engraver, Robert Scott (1777–1841). He moved to London at the age of 26 and later moved to Newcastle on Tyne, in northeastern England. His best work was in the Pre-Raphaelite style, with scenes from Northumberland history.
PAGES 344, 354

KOYANAGUI SEI
[b. 1896, death date unknown]
PAGES 170, 202

ADA SHIRLEY-FOX
[fl. c. 1888–1914]
English painter who specialized in figurative subjects and portraits. After studying in Paris, she married John Shirley-Fox and lived in Bath, England.
PAGES 82–83

RAJA UMED SINGH OF KOTAH
[1771–1819]
PAGE 315, 328–29

HUNT SLONEM
[b. 1951]
American painter whose grand-scale canvases and intimate baroque works explore exotica. He shares his vast loft space with aviaries that house his primary subjects, tropical birds. His work ranges from monumental, richly colored masses of birds to the sensuous rendering of saints, mysterious figures, and exotic animals.
PAGES 166–67, 266, 292–93, 371

LO SPAGNA
(GIOVANNI DI PIETRO SPAGNA)
[c. 1450–1528]
PAGES 376–77

PHILIP WILSON STEER
[1860–1942]
British painter who was a founder of the New English Art Club when he was 26. He traveled to France and was profoundly influenced by the Impressionists. He was in his prime around the turn of the century, painting beach scenes, seascapes, and interiors that were full of brilliant light.
PAGES 38–39

THÉOPHILE-ALEXANDRE STEINLEN
[1859–1923]
Swiss artist born in Lausanne, although he moved to Paris in his twenties and settled in Montmartre. He worked in oils, pastel, and other media to produce scenes of the teeming life of the area. Among these works were many lithographs of street and cabaret life and posters advertising items such as sterilized milk and veterinary services. Steinlen was passionately concerned about animals, especially the local cats, which he drew with immense skill, capturing the fleeting moments in their lives.
PAGES 22, 64–65, 66–68, 84–85, 132–33, 151, 180, 196, 234, 245, 267, 277

ALYSSE STEPANIAN
[b. 1961]
Iranian artist now living in the US who is known for her performance art as well as her canvases, which interweave abstraction with figuration. She has exhibited in the US, Spain, and Armenia.
PAGES 55, 73

GEORGE STUBBS
[1724–1806]
English painter and printmaker whose study of anatomy led to accurate paintings of horses, dogs, and wild animals, for which he was well known in his lifetime. Somewhat suprisingly, he was virtually self-taught as a painter. Early in his career he earned his living mainly as a portraitist and was sought after by the aristocracy, but he could also paint grooms and servants with touching authority. As well as being truthful to nature, his works displayed a great talent for design and composition.
PAGE 105

Frank ROMERO
Scamp in a Snow Flurry (1995)

NICOLAS TARKHOFF
[1871–1930]
Russian artist.
PAGES 169, 192

HANS THOMA
[1839–1924]
German painter, printmaker, and museum director. During the 1870s

he became interested in mythology and symbolism and subsequently found increasing popular support, particularly at the Munich Kunstverein exhibition of 1890. In 1899 he became director of the Kunsthalle in Karlsruhe and thereafter exhibited frequently.
PAGES 345, 355, 366–67

GIULIO DEL TORRE
[1856–1932]
PAGES 302–303

HENRI DE TOULOUSE-LAUTREC
[1864–1901]
French painter and printmaker best known for his scenes of nineteenth-century Parisian life. He enjoyed great success during his lifetime. Like many artists of his period, he lived a Bohemian lifestyle in an impoverished area of Paris, which brought shame on his aristocratic family.
PAGE 294

CHARLES TOWNE
[1763–1840]
English artist who specialized in landscape and animal paintings. He exhibited at the Royal Academy and elsewhere.
PAGES 254–55

WILLIAM HENRY HAMILTON TROOD
[1860–99]
English animal painter, particularly of dogs, whose paintings usually have sentimental titles.
PAGES 168, 171, 178–79, 206, 209, 214–16

SUZANNE VALADON
[1867–1938]
French painter and mother of Maurice Utrillo (1883–1955). After working as a dishwasher and artists' model, she began to paint seriously with the encouragement of Pierre-Auguste Renoir (1841–1919) and Edgar Degas (1834–1917). Her figure painting was notable for very strong coloring and energy, and she was strongly influenced by the work of Edgar Degas.
PAGES 268, 282

DONATO VENEZIANO
[fl. 1344–82]
PAGE 346, 368–69

NICOLAS OF VERDUN
[fl. 1150–1200]
Dutch painter and worker in enamel and metal. His altarpieces still exist in many churches in Austria, France, and Germany, notably the Shrine of the Three Kings in the Cologne Cathedral.
PAGE 356

JAN CORNELISZ VERMEYEN
[c. 1500–59]
Dutch painter and tapestry designer said to be a pupil of Jan Gossaert (called Mabuse, c. 1478–c. 1533), he was the court painter to Margaret of Austria (1480–1530), regent of The Netherlands. In 1535 he went to North Africa with Emperor Charles V (1500–58) and painted images featuring the scenery there.
PAGE 69

SIMON DE VOS
[1603–76]
Flemish painter born in Antwerp. Influenced by Peter Paul Rubens (1577–1640) and Sir Anthony van Dyck (1599–1641), he painted many religious and genre scenes.
PAGES 350–51

LOUIS WAIN
[1860–1939]
English artist with some French ancestry. He became very much the "man who drew cats." His drawings, paintings, and lithographs illustrated many Catland Annuals and he produced countless postcards. Wain depicted cats performing all kinds of human activity, and later he portrayed cats in human clothing but still engaged in the same activities. Wain's mental health worsened, and he was eventually committed to an asylum, where he continued to paint increasingly bizarre animals. A fund was raised to enable him to move to a more comfortable hospital, where he died having completed a series of "psychedelic" works.
PAGES 12, 45

SAMUEL WALKER
[1802–74]
PAGES 16–17

Jonathan BURKE
Habitat (1998)

Christian PIERRE
Young Tiger (late 20th Century)

ALFRED WARD
[fl. 1873–1927]
English genre painter who exhibited at the Royal Academy from 1873 onward, and elsewhere.
PAGE 301

JAMES WARD
[1769–1859]
English painter and engraver, considered by many as the most important animal painter of his generation. His work epitomises Romanticism with animated animals, sweeping landscapes, and dramatic skies. He was a frequent exhibitor at the British Institution and the Royal Academy.
PAGE 122

ARTHUR WARDLE
[1864–1949]
English animal painter who specialized in both domestic and wild animals (and sports scenes), using pastel and watercolor. He made many wonderful animal studies and an exhibition of his work took place in 1935 at the Vicars Gallery. He also exhibited at the Royal Academy from 1880 to 1935.
PAGES 332–34

ROBERT WARRENS
[b. 1933]
Contemporary American artist, Warrens has taught at Louisiana State University since 1967. He has completed murals for the Katz and Besthoff Collection, the Pan American building, and the Aquarium of the Americas, all in New Orleans where he now lives, and for the Centroplex Building in Baton Rouge.
PAGES 12, 49

MARGO WEINSTEIN
[20th Century]
Contemporary American artist Weinstein depicts archetypal imagery in Interior Zoo, part of an ongoing photographic exploration of the subject. She believes that the animals that inhabit the human psyche visit us bearing messages, which in our increasingly technological age we ignore at our peril. If, however, we honor them, we may greatly enrich our lives by connecting with unknown aspects of ourselves.
PAGE 149

BENJAMIN WEST
[1738–1820]
American painter who was born in Philadelphia but worked mainly in England. He broke new ground by depicting a recent historical scene "The Death of Wolfe" in contemporary clothing. He became president of the Royal Academy with the patronage of King George III (1738–1820).
PAGES 198–99

C. WILSON
[fl. 19th Century]
PAGES 15, 28–29

MARIAN WINSRYG
[b. 1941]
American artist based in Los Angeles. She is widely known as a portraitist of domestic animals. Her paintings combine social commentary and humor, frequently using animals as the principal players.
PAGE 111

WILLIAM WOODHOUSE
[1857–1935]
PAGES 160–61

JOACHIM WTEWAEL
[1566–1638]
Dutch artist born in Utrecht who painted in the exaggerated Mannerist fashion. After traveling in Italy and France, he created many religious subjects in a rather contorted style.
PAGES 232, 246

EUGENIO ZAMPIGHI
[1859–1944]
PAGES 144–45

JOHANN ZOFFANY
[1733–1810]
German artist who settled in England at the age of 26. He made his name as a painter of theatrical scenes and figures such as the actor and dramatist David Garrick (1717–79). Later genre and conversation pieces attracted the attention of the royal family. His self-portraits are engaging in their slight self-mockery.
PAGES 268, 294–95